The Journey of the Soul

The Journey of the Soul

H. I. Mavioglu

iUniverse, Inc.
New York Lincoln Shanghai

The Journey of the Soul

iUniverse, Inc.

For information address:
iUniverse, Inc.
2021 Pine Lake Road, Suite 100
Lincoln, NE 68512
www.iuniverse.com

ISBN: 0-595-30556-3

Printed in the United States of America

Acknowledgement

A poet dips his cup into the well of creativity; fills it before dipping his pen into an inkwell. When he is ready to compose, he retrieves his cup only to find that most of its content has evaporated, except a few drops at the bottom, enough to recreate the rhythm, the sound and the beauty of poetry.

I am grateful to many:

To the child who threw a pebble into a pond and watched the ripples in wonder, for to wonder is to sow the seeds of wisdom—

To the first person who opened the human mind and spirit by performing the first impossible task of uttering the first word—

To the person who spun the first tale around the campfire, who composed the first song and merrily sang it to celebrate an occasion—

To the person who composed the first vague invocation and chanted it to please the gods above—

To the places I have been and to the people I have met—

To the others I have not met, but seeing their paths, I found my own—

To the unknown bard who composed the first lay without attaching his name to it—

To the names from Sih-liqu-unninni to Homer, from Homer to N. D. Walsch, and every known name who came before, after, and those yet to come—

To my friends who helped me over the years at different phases of this epic: Susan and Don Barnes, N.H.I. Basho, Andrea Cook, Tamara Degotz, Filiz and Aykut Edibali, Thomas Kavadias, Grace R. Long, Joyce, Nesli, and Kurt

Mavioglu, Richard Meister Jr., Kira and Mike Mirsky, Pat Pfeiffer, Christa Richardson, Filiz Satir and Ayshen Yuksel.

H. I. Mavioglu

Table of Contents

I.   The Invisible Shells

A child is born as an individual
With an inimitable Self and Soul:
No stigma of the original sin,
No prejudice of the mature man.

A child is more than a source of happiness
And fulfillment given to his parents.
Parenting is more than a daily duty,
For giving care to a child is the same
As giving care to whole humanity.
He is more than a repository
For the genes of his mother and father
To pass on to future generations.
Therefore creating an illusion that
Genes are a form of immortality.

A new born baby's true identity
Is never identified and acknowledged.
People would not say, "Here comes an infant
Who is a new guest from Eternity,
And a new enrollee in the Earth School."

When a child is born, his umbilical
Cord turns into a useless appendage,
And it is cut at once by someone else.
What's left behind is a visible scar,
Which hints to us that a vital lifeline
Can turn into a liability
By leaving a weak spot to cause hernia
Or to collect lint all through one's lifetime.

Soon after the baby's first breath of air
It's classified as a boy or a girl,
And then swaddled with invisible shells
Of nationality, color, country
Of origin, religion, superstitions,
Customs, and prejudices of its clan.

Every culture masters the art of melting
The minds of its children and pouring them
Into misshapen molds of their own design.

The mold of prejudice is the worst one,
For it teaches a child how to condemn
His playmates without giving them a chance
To foster a friendship among themselves.
Yet no one knows how to shatter that mold.

Without child's consent he becomes a Christian,
A Muslim, a Buddhist or a Hindu.
Faiths are neither wholly holy nor evil,
Neither essential nor dispensable.
Yet these invisible shells insulate
The Self so the energy of the Soul
Can't flow into the Self to energize
It to grow into a *Transcendent Self*.
Without a Transcendent Self, one cannot
Extend to reach beyond the Planet Earth.

Invisible shells have tentacles,
Which are attached to the individual
And to the society one lives in,
For shells need dual sources of nourishment.

As a child grows into maturity,
He will have accumulated more layers
Of invisible shells in the nature
Of fear, anxiety, jealousy, and envy.
Thus the Self becomes sluggish and earthly.

The origin of *the mortal Self* is the Earth.
Self consists of *a body and brain complex*
With five senses to function on this Earth.
The Self must toil to earn its daily bread
To nurse itself and, inevitably,
It must return to its origin.

The source of the *immortal Soul* is God.
The Soul must hold a universal love,
And teach this unselfish love to the Self.
Having done this, it can unite with God.

The Soul and Self are meant to align with
Each other to form the Transcendent Self,
In which the Soul and Self are in accord,
But the mortal Self and the immortal
Soul are different in purpose and goal.

The Self has an inborn leaning to turn
Into a bottomless pit that cannot
Be filled by stuffing it with needs and wants.
As soon as its basic needs of a mate
And meals are satisfied, then instantly,
The Self hungers and hankers for more mates
And meals that it can't use in many lifetimes.

The brain thinks, reasons, and deliberates,
But it can fool itself by assuming
That what it deeply desires is the truth.
It will know that a limb is amputated,
Yet long after will feel the phantom pain.

The Soul has no needs. It's a whole by itself.
It needs to learn nothing in this Earth School.
Still it wants to perceive itself through Self.

Thus the unity of Soul and Self may
Not happen naturally in one lifetime.
To bring that about both must work together,

And the Self must learn to decrease its needs,
For the Soul won't force its will on the Self.

To people, the Self is perceptible.
They'll go to any length meeting Self's needs.
And for them the Soul is an abstract thought.
They cannot fathom what that immortal
Soul ought to teach the Self in one's lifetime.

Unlike the umbilical cord, someone's
Accumulated invisible shells
Can't be cut or shelled by somebody else.
Each person must shed his invisible
Shells exclusively by his own efforts
To align the Soul and the Self to bring about
Harmony and accord between the two.
Thus the Self can evolve into a Transcendent
Self and can embrace universal love.
So the perfect circle is complete.
There is no more Self or Soul; they are One.

When one enters into the *State of Oneness,*
One has attained the ultimate level
Of existence for which one was aiming.

The veil is lifted from the face of Truth.
Now, one is in an *Eternal Time Zone.*
In that sanctified moment one will be
One with the Eternal One here and now.

A circle has no beginning, no end.
Thus a circle is the symbol of God.
A proper pronoun for God is never
He, She or It but a capital O.

II.   The Fate of Beings

As men, beasts, ants, and bees live their short lives,
They do what they have been programmed to do.
They repeat the same tasks all through their lives.
They have no power to change their own fate,
Much less to change the fate of other beings.

Then a dauntless bee dares to break the rules
By flying farther than any other
Bee has ever flown before to collect
Pollen from a healing herb not only
To feed the body but also the Soul.
And a man dares to dive deeper into
His Inner-self to reach beyond himself.

When it's time for a worldly man to go,
Having no ties with the rest of the cosmos,
He attempts to leave his footprints behind.
But the curtain of time will conceal them.
Hence future generations will never
Detect that the footprints were ever there.

When a person with a Transcendent Self
Is set to go, knowing where he is going,
He leaves nothing behind him but an empty
Space for the use of future generations.

A man who can see everything remains
Invisible, for he's not apart from
Anything but is a part of everything.

III.   Government and Men

There were people before there was a government.
The people were free to do anything
They wanted to do without hurting others.
Predatory instincts of the people
Were controlled by customs and taboos.

As the people multiplied, they formed tribes.
As they accumulated property,
Criminal elements started to grow.
To protect the property and safety
Of the people they fashioned a government
By curbing individual liberties.

To be viable, a living thing must
Be born with all of its vital organs.
Yet one of its unvital appendage
May grow faster than an inherent one.
As the horns start to grow after the ears
And get stronger and longer than the ears.
Though government was designed as an appendage,
From the beginning, it led an unyielding
Life of its own by trying to be stronger
Than the people it was to serve and shelter.

Moral codes changed in favor of government.
When a person committed a murder,
It was still an abominable crime.
When a government committed a murder,
By capital punishment, it was legal.
Thus a remedy turned into a bane.

H. I. Mavioglu

Criminal elements from each tribe crossed
The borders of the other tribe to steal
Its goods, and to kidnap and rape its women.
When the tribes went to war, it was never
Fought just between criminal elements,
But between the honest men of each tribe,
Thus one tribe's honest men killing the next
Tribe's honest men became acceptable.
Though these men would have preferred to visit
Each other in their festive days to talk,
Sing and dance together by the fireside.

When the first ruler took his first sip from
The elixir of power, he became
Instantly addicted to its flavor.
He did not want to relinquish his power,
Even after his death. Thereby establishing
A hereditary form of monarchy.

When the people found out that they could not
Rely on their government for their safety,
They invoked the invisible powers
To help them, which gave birth to religion.

The ruler usurped this invisible
Power as well to rule over the people
Not just–*here and now*–but also–*hereafter*-.
Thus theocracy reigned its reign of terror.

There can be no just government in a country
Where its people practice warped moral codes.
Just laws can't guarantee an honest government.
You show me a land where shopkeepers cheat,
And people don't pay their fair share of taxes,
There I will show you a corrupt government.

The power is the property of people.
They may entrust their power willingly,
Or it may be snatched from their hands by force.

Still they reserve the right to take it back:
Peacefully, if it won't work forcefully.

At this stage of human development,
We still are in need of a lawful government.
It should be elected by the people
For the creation of social conditions
For all to reach their highest potentials.

Government should respect not only the rights
Of the majority and minorities
But also the rights of one man who stands
Within the laws but at the fringes
Of the conventional society.

Above all I do not want any form
Of government to endorse or censure my,
Or my neighbor's, personal belief system.
It does not hurt me, if my neighbor were
To believe in one God, or in thousands
Of gods, or believe in no God at all.

I do not want any government that could
Corrupt the morality of my youth
By hinting that youth can be rude to their
Neighbors without feeling any remorse.

When men raise themselves to a height where they
Are not motivated by their egotism,
And can find happiness in core values,
Then they'll govern themselves without a government.

The wealth of government runs like a river:
With its overflowing springtime runoff,
Trickling summer flow, and hard winter freeze.
It won't take its headwaters from the peaks,
And its tributaries from the highlands.
Unlike a river, it won't form a lake,
Or a reservoir that could be used during
A drought, but it evaporates before

It can reach and wet the parched and cracked lips
Of the lowlands, much less reach the oceans.

Just to meet the bare needs of the lowlands,
Government digs deep into the viscera
Of the lowlands to tap the hidden pockets.

IV.   Historical Events and Men

Historical happenings of the first
Magnitude to influence the people's lives
Seldom happen. Men soon smooth down
The jagged edges of events and turn
Them into harmless or heroic tales.

We remember Harry S. Truman not
For Hiroshima and Nagasaki,
But for being the president in office
When the Japanese Empire was defeated,
And consequently bloodshed was ended.
We honor him not for being the victor,
But for extending his hands and the hands
Of all Americans toward the vanquished,
Not to plunder but to set them upright,
So they could recast their affairs in peace.

We remember Eisenhower not as
A war hero, but as a peacemaker,
For he was the president in office
When the killing in Korea was over.

V.　　　**War and Men**

War is an inborn madness of mankind.
It may skip a generation or two.
Still that bad gene clings to men's DNA
In recessive mode waiting to wake up.
Abruptly, it appears with all its fury,
Unless mankind can elevate himself
To a higher level of enlightenment
To overcome that genetic aberrance.

The war of the people is much more than
A contention over territory.
Wild beasts can do this better than men can.
But only men can carefully plan, plot,
And prepare to wage war over his kind.
Once they decide to fight they find a cause.
It may be over a land, or vengeance.
Then they claim that their cause is a just one,
And each side claims that God is on their side,
As if God had ever blessed any war.

One can't say any good comes through a war,
Yet it brings down the barriers and shatters
The shells of both the winners and the losers,
And brings them in contact in a way that
It would never be possible in peacetime.

War slays the fire-breathing dragons and mellows
The unwavering keepers of the temples,
Takes the temple gates off their hinges, opens
Holes in their walls for people to pass through.

War allows people to pick up trinkets
As souvenir and unknowingly or
Knowingly let them leave something behind.
It allows them to become acquainted
With each other as fellow human beings,
And lets them infuse life into each other.
There is no destructive force on Earth that
Is strong enough to block the flow of life.

VI.   The Fifties

The fifties was one of those historic
Periods that was most favorable
For the citizens of America.
Hunger pains of the Depression were just
A fictitious tale on the tongues of folks.
Traditional family ties were intact.
The deep wounds of World War II were well healed.
The oozing blood of the Korean War
Was not enough to cause anemia.
There was no bloodstain on the US mainland.

Selective forgetfulness was taking
Place and helping in the healing process.
Without spontaneous tears, mothers were
Beginning to remember and proudly talk
Of the happy days of their fallen sons.

The widows of the slain soldiers were married
Again, and they were rearing sons and daughters,
And refusing to consider that they
Might lose them in the conflicts yet to come.

After having witnessed her firstborn torn
To pieces by coyotes, a young doe will
Conceive and fawn again spring after spring.

Historically wealth has always been kept
In check by a select few while the masses
Survived at or near poverty lines.
However, in the fifties a middle
Class was growing and making a good living.

Thus reversing the historical trend
Of distribution of wealth among people.
The masses were dreaming powerful dreams.
It was a special time for hope to blossom
And gloom and despair to remain dormant.
The cold winds of the cold war were still stirring,
But people were already acclimated.

VII. The Cultural Exchange in the Fifties

The cultural exchange was in full swing.
In any teaching hospital one half
Of the house staff were foreign physicians.
Those ambitious young interns were learning
Through healing the sick of America.

These interns were unlike the immigrants
Who came before them from their countries.

Majority of earlier immigrants
Were of the lowest level of their countries:
The poorest, the despised and the rejected.
They came with a plan to shed their Old World
Selfhood and be reborn to a new life.
They were also automatically
Equipped with an unbounded capacity
To imitate and adopt the new ways.
To secure success these men had to blend
In with fellow men; do as others do,
Learn the lingo, and play the game to win.

The interns were the cream of their countries,
And the majority of them were sponsored
By the universities of their countries.
Their progress in the U.S. was monitored.
They were to be selective as to what
They ought to learn also what not to learn.
As they learned, they ought not to forget who
They were, and where their roots were imbedded.

Like Prometheus they were to steal the fire
Of science and take it back to their countries.

The house staff room was their finest classroom.
They would present their cases to each other,
Tell what they had done already, and ask
What more could be done for their patients.

They would warn each other about a certain
Sadistic night nurse who would fabricate
A frivolous reason to call the interns
During the middle of the night, and watch
Them stagger and hold on to bedposts like
Drunkards, dazed due to sleep deprivation.
They would also, warn each other about
A kindly old surgeon who would promise
That he will allow them to operate.
Instead he'd let them pull retractors through
Their rotation without letting them cut.

Hearing the multitude of languages
Spoken in the interns' lounge, one might think
That one was in the Tower of Babel.
In contrast to the people of the Tower,
These interns could converse and understand
Each other in multiple languages.
Their goal was not to erect together
One shared tall tower to reach the heavens.
Each intern had plans to build his own tower.

They would begin to converse in English.
Soon they would switch to their native language.
Then to the languages of other interns.
One intern would be conversing in five
Different languages at the same time.

One female intern used to say, "I am
Fluent in many tongues but I can't speak
In any one of them *without* an accent.
I've billions of neurons to learn to speak,

But one pair of vocal cords to pronounce;
So as the words come out they sound the same."

They sought to speak unaccented English.
One would say, "Hey, you are a genius,
Why don't you find a technique that will make
It possible to transfer a dying
Patient's English to a living intern?"
The answer, "I'm not interested in that,
I'd like to find a way that will make it
Possible for me to finish my work
And will provide me with some time to sleep."
Austin, an American intern, would
Remind the Europeans that they were luckier
Than their Oriental colleagues for they
Did not have to begin with the alphabet.

The interns were a goal-directed group.
They also dared to dream. Their dreams would start
Back home, might have some scenes from America,
Once more their dreams would quicken to go back
To home to come full circle to come through.
The dreams of interns would run parallel
To each other's without overlapping.

How little did they know that their unattended
And deserted dreams, in their native land,
Were being stunted by each passing day.

VIII. Each Foreign Intern Had a Tale to Tell

Each foreign intern had a tale to tell.
They had invisible but painful scars,
For they were branded with the brand of war.
Yet these strong-willed young interns were not willing
To be branded as victims or survivors.

Germany was in ruins and divided.
The feelings of the Germans were discordant.
Schutz of East Germany could not endure
To live any longer than a few days
In the house staff quarters, for it
Reminded him of the refugee camps.

Liebig talked about how his family,
And his neighbors had been forced to get out
Of Czechoslovakia, for no other
Reason than they happened to be Germans.

Leibniz was emotional. She would confess
That each time she would face a veteran
She'd find herself asking, "Is this the man
Who bombed German cities down to the ground?
Is he the one who killed German children?"

Lietz was expressive and outspoken;
For him Deutschland was down but never out.
Her military machinery was
Silenced, but not the spirits of her scientists.
He'd say, "Only with the help of second
Rate German scientists, and American

Atomic information leaks, the Russians
Built the atomic bomb in forty-nine.
Thus ending the four years of American
Monopoly over the atomic bomb.
Because of this monopoly, Russia
Could not hold in bondage all of Europe.
The Russians, with their resources, could not
Have split anything if it could not be
Split with a huge sledgehammer and a wedge."

When his voice would change and sound as if he
Were reciting poetry, then interns
Would surmise that his next topic would be
The space exploration. "German science
And technology will give wings to mankind.
And as men penetrate deeper into
The boundless heavens, they will evolve into
The next stage of human evolution.
As they look down on the Earth, they will say,
'There is our birthplace but not our jailhouse.'"

Deguchi was an enigma hidden
In the labyrinths of his inner space.
No one could read his feelings from his facial
Expressions, for his face was a blank page.
Either he did not have feelings,
Or deliberately enshrouded them.
He vented not a word about the war,
Victory, defeat or the occupation,
For the first time in Japan's history.
He whispered not a single word about
The atomic bomb or Hiroshima
Or the Japanese attack on Pearl Harbor.

In time, a few words leaked out of his mouth.
When he was coming to America,
His professor had reprimanded him,
"Go away and don't bother to come back.
Vanquished Japan can no longer afford
To harbor her irresolute young men!"

Once again he said, "When people address
Me by my first name, I feel as if my
Privacy is being violated.
In Japan only parents and elder
Members of the clan have the privilege
Of calling a person by his first name."

He would be either sleeping or working.
However, it was hard to tell whether
He had been sleeping more or working more.
At the end of the year when he published
More papers than the rest, the case was closed.

Lee would talk about how North Koreans
Killed her family, confiscated their
Properties, and how she escaped with nothing
But a diploma to the South Korea.

Hegedus would add, "There is no North or
South Hungary for people to escape.
The whole country is run by the by Russians
And they act like the masters of the land."

Adem Ademoglu kept mostly quiet
While other foreign interns would complain
About the hardships that they had encountered.
He was born and raised in Turkiye during
A period of peace. The war was not
A determining factor in his life.
He innocently believed that one gets
Out of life what one had put into it.

IX. Generalizations and the Common Bonds

While trying to get to know a group, judging
That group by its weakest individual,
And then generalizing his weaknesses,
And projecting them on the rest is unfair.
But getting to know an individual,
On his own merits, is too difficult,
Even an impossible task to tackle.
It is easy to classify Spanish
Speaking interns as Spaniards regardless
Of their race or country of origin
And say, "Spaniards act this way or that way."
Who has time to find out who Jose is?
Who cares to know his strengths or weaknesses?

These young women and men interns
Were bright, sharp, dedicated and fiercely
Competitive, and wore the same white coats.
Their common enemy was death itself.
Their souls were at risk. They fought at all hours
Of the day and night, and willingly will
Continue to battle all through their lives.

Surely they knew death was invincible,
Still they put faith in the fact that giving
One extra brilliant moment was worth giving.

Medicine was not an exact science.
Each therapeutic intervention was
A new trial for each individual.

By making an exact diagnosis,
And by providing the proper therapy
One could not guarantee the same outcome.
Some would be cured while some others could not.

After doing everything, a physician
Might still lose, and his soul searching could not
Give an answer that would apply to all.
He had to learn to live with uncertainties.
He had to learn that people were ennobled
By their sufferings; had to learn from them.

Kinship among these interns was fostered
Through the same ordeals that they have gone through.
Regardless of their national origins,
The interns were members of the same clan.
They were the disciples of Apollo,
The Healer, who taught healing art to men.
They were under the Hippocratic oath.

Soon national lines were crossed, and they started
To know each other as individuals.

X.   The American Interns

The American interns were either
World War II or Korean War veterans.
There were no draft-dodgers in the fifties.
They were more fortunate than their foreign
Colleagues, for they left behind the destruction
And reminders of war in foreign countries.

In general, the American interns
Looked homogeneous because they started
From the same starting block, covered the same
Distance, and their finish line was in sight.
Some of them were planning to practice
In nearby towns; Kirkwood, Maryland Heights,
University City, or Clayton,
While others were planning to go into
Academic medicine at the same
Institutions where they were being trained.
They were journeying on the smooth section
Of the trail: no peaks or canyons ahead.

Most of them were married, and their spouses
Were supplementing their GI benefits.

They were encouraged to foster free thoughts,
And to express their ideas freely.
Also their minds were carefully conditioned,
So that they knew what was proper to say.

Their concept of culture consisted of:
Listening to classical music while
They were relaxing, attending concerts,

Operas, plays and an occasional ballet.
They were just the consumers of culture.
They had no inclination to acquire
Culture by studying literature.
Foreign language literacy was not
Important for them, and the cultures of
Other nations were just a curiosity.

Among the American interns, Joe
Davis, Alan Edmonton and Charlie
Nelson stood out as individuals.

Joe Davis was a man who quickly passed
Through the skin and touched the hearts of people.
He worked methodically: neither lagged
Behind nor went all out to get ahead.
For him it was not outer covering
Nor containers but the content that counted.
He was not quite satisfied by hearing
The vibrations of people's vocal cords.
He tuned to the vibrations of their souls.

He had a warm smile but one could detect
A well-concealed sadness beneath that smile.
He was so helpful to the foreign interns:
Which department store was the best to shop?
Which medical bookstore stocked interns handbooks?
What time was the best time to call back home
To get the most economical rates?

In the early fifties malpractice suits
Were starting to be filed, which was affecting
The patient/physician relationship.

To minimize the risk factors that might
Catch the physicians off guard and to lessen
The chances of the lawyers to sue them,
Organized medicine was assuring
The physicians, they were not legally

Bound to provide care to anybody
Who was not already under their care.

Thus if a physician happens to see
An emergency case in public places,
He might legally sneak from the scene.
If he were to do that, would he be able
To walk away from his private judgement
Without feeling guilty in his conscious?

Hospital liability insurance
Was covering interns in the hospital.
If they were to help a patient outside
Of a hospital they were on their own.

Joe was a genuine Good Samaritan.
The consequences of the medical
Liability laws did not daunt him.
Wherever his help was needed, he stopped.
When it was necessary, he loaded
Sick or injured people into his car
And rushed them to the emergency room.

One night he was working in the ER,
Just before twelve-midnight, there came a young
Lady who had been involved in a wreck,
And her face had been pushed through the windshield.
She suffered no head injury or broken
Facial bones, but her face was cut to pieces.

Even though his hectic shift was over,
He would not walk out and let the next shift
Do what they could do for her pretty face.
He sat on a stool, and put the pieces
Of the shredded skin into their places,
And stitched them together with finest silk.
After four hours of work all the pieces
Of the jigsaw puzzle fitted together.

The next afternoon the young lady paid
A visit to thank him, and said that she
Had consulted with her plastic surgeon
Who said that the reconstruction was flawless,
Given time for the healing to take place.

The healing art consists of skill and care.
Skill is an acquired capability.
Care is a connatural quality.
Joe was born with the spirit of a healer.

When foreign interns chattered about their
Cities, he would listen attentively,
And would ask quick questions about minute
Details, and would take mental notes as though
He were planning a trip to Istanbul,
Salonika, Berlin or Tokyo.
So that if he were to visit those places
He would not miss a thing and feel at home.

Before long Joe finished his internship,
Joe's sister, Peggy, called Adem and said,
"Joe had died. You are one of his pallbearers.
Joe will be missed by all who had known him,
But death did not take him without a warning.
During his last year of medical school
He had an acute form of leukemia.
After treatments, he went into remission
Which allowed him to finish his internship.
He realized his prognosis was dismal,
Yet chose to extract life out of each moment."

When one has a short way to go and too
Much to experience, why should one rush?

Alan would have been Alan wherever
He was born, and whatever his race was.
He could see only the surface layer,
Which gave him an ability to see
The blemishes on the epithelial

Layer of anybody else's smooth skin.
If his fair complexion were to belong
To someone else he could've found many flaws.
He was lucky to find a beauty in himself
That he could not find in anybody else.

He was not shy to say, "I hate to go
To a conference where a foreign intern
Is presenting a case. It's a waste of time.
In my mind I'd be correcting his accent.
When I come out of the conference room,
I realize that I have retained nothing."

When Alan was jilted by one girlfriend
After another and saw them fall into
The arms of the accented foreign interns,
He could not grasp that love sings just love's songs
By feeling the beats without caring whether
The lyrics are in English or Turkish.

He became a skilful surgeon who saw
Blood, bones, muscles, guts and organs beneath
The skin but found no soul in anyone.
Through his skills he made a fortune and owned
The best things that only money could buy.

Who can hope to find genuine happiness
In the illusive glitter of the world?
Happiness is a merely a reflection
Of one's Inner Light, which cast outwardly.
How could one connect with another's soul?
If one were not in touch with one's own soul.

Charlie Nelson was the oldest intern.
He might not have been the wisest intern,
Though he was wise enough not to stereotype
People but see them as individuals.
He had no room in his heart for whiners.

For him, men's accomplishments and failures
Were nothing but reflections of their choices.
All through history even slaves had choices.

First, he had obtained a Ph.D. in
International political science.
Soon he became disappointed with politics
Of any kind and switched to medicine.

His piercing eyes focused on the men's core.
His large frame and brawny build assured one
That he was well anchored and would not drift.

His unorthodox ideas would not
Change in line with popular perceptions.
One who can focus at the core of concepts,
Can't be sidetracked by their outwardly meanings.

XI.   Adem Ademoglu

Adem was one of those foreign interns.
I will tell his story first for it is
Shorter than that of the other interns.
He lost no country, was chased from nowhere,
No member of his clan was killed in war.
He had to finish his postdoctoral
Program at some place and the United
States was a proper country to do so.

He remembered St. Louis of the fifties
Not for its beauty, but for its high spirits.
The air was gray; yet no one called it smog.
For Adem the city was no more than
A container that held the hospital;
Concert halls, restaurants, and sport arenas
Of the city offered nothing for him.

His goals were buried in the operating
Rooms, wards, conference rooms, and libraries.
It was a six-year program, but during
His first year he learned all he had to learn.
The rest of his education gave him skills.

He left his heart with his fiancée, Nuran,
Though he thought his body and mind were still
Strong and fit to focus on his studies.
He already knew that the brain can reason
And can compromise. Was he now finding
Out that the soul can embrace or reject?

He was distracted and missing things that
He never imagined were important.
Living on a prairie without a ring
Of mountains around it was like living
In a glass house without privacy.
He was feeling exposed and stark-naked.
He was missing the upward winding trails,
Leading him to the crest of a high peak,
Which allowed him to have a bird's eye view
Of the green valley below, and gave him
A sense that he was closer to the heavens.

He was missing box canyons to sing into
And to hear them echo, and to feel that
Nature was aware of his existence,
Thus he was an integral part of all.
He was longing for the thyme scented clear
Air of the foothills of Mt. Erciyes.

1. Kalaycik Canyon

To lighten the pressures of his present
Problems, his mind shifted back to his boyhood.
He found himself in the Kalaycik Canyon.
He was picnicking with his childhood friends.
The high cliffs were standing guard at both sides
Of the Canyon and giving an impression
That it was a safe and secluded place.
At the middle of it, a stream was rushing
And giving life to the valley below.
Weeping willows were hanging loose on both
Shores of the stream, and providing homes for
The birds, and shade for the sake of picnickers.

The boys' eyes were studying the sheer cliff
Walls of the canyon for every fissure
And every toe hole as they'd done before.
For the challenge and the key to manhood
Were hidden in those cracks and tiny holes.

A large flock of wild doves nested and lived
Their lives in those cliffs, and raised their young ones.

As the boys would picnic and cool themselves
In the stream, doves would dance the dance of courtship,
Sing the song of love and feed the hungry
Squabs, and soar high to dance the dance of life.
Suddenly, a falcon would speed towards
The frolicking flock, and the doves would panic,
Then the dance of survival would take over,
And feathers would fly as the falcon's claws
Are clasped around a dove—no time to mourn.
Quickly normal flow of life would resume.

A falcon earns that day's flesh for its chicks,
And the squabs in the dove's nest slowly starve.

Those boys were spectators in a life drama.
They would neither glorify the falcon,
For its lightning-like swiftness and courage,
Nor would they grieve for the fate of the dove.
They must have surmised that life thrives on life.

2. The Dervishes

After the picnic the boys went upstream
And arrived at their hidden swimming hole.
After swimming for a while, they headed
Up to the source of the stream in the cave.
At every summer solstice, the dervishes
Would hold their rituals in the same cave.
The boys happened to choose the same day for
Their picnic, so that they had a free show.

The dervishes warmed up themselves by fire walking.
They heated their cymbals over the coals,
And as they played, they pressed the hot cymbals
On their bare chests without being blistered.

When one thought that the show was over
The music would grow more mysterious.
They enjoyed the music of each instrument,
But the tune of the flute enriched their souls.

They built their flutes out of natural reed.
As they played, they felt that their souls were making
The tune, for the breath was coming from within.

When the flute hit the high note, the dervishes
Sprang to dance by whirling counterclockwise.
All through the dance they maintained the same pose.
Their right hands were raised toward the heavens,
Their left hands were lowered toward the Earth,
As if they were symbolically bridging
The gap between the cosmos and the Earth.

They kept their hands open to show that they
Were neither keeping anything for themselves,
Nor were they grabbing at anything worldly,
But were free agents in the universe.

Suddenly, the music stopped. For a moment
They stood still, but the next moment they sat
On the floor of the cave, and formed a circle.
As they rocked rhythmically back-and-forth,
They chanted hymns with their bellow-like lungs.
As they'd suck in and let out the damp air,
They produced a universal music.

The boys could not understand their prayers,
But felt the mysterious vibrations.
When the spirituals of the dervishes
Created an eerie air, the boys felt
Uneasy and they returned to the cliffs.

3. Cliff Climbing

At the cliffs, they grew calm and calculating.
They knew the rules of the game: no daring,
No encouragement, or discouragement.
Either one of the boys would step forward
On his own or they would return to town.
On that day Adem stepped forward to climb.

No safety measures: no harness, no ropes,
No thought of the distance to the hospital.
The driving force was the lure of the cliffs.
A boy had to climb up those perilous
Cliffs to borrow a couple wild dove eggs
As a trophy, and descend as a man,
Or plummet and die on the rocky grounds.

Adem was on his way up the sheer cliff,
Clinging with one hand and taking a couple
Of eggs from a nest with the other hand.
He put the eggs into a small charm pouch
Around his neck, and started to descend.
Some boys were holding their breath and watching,
Some boys were holding their breath but not watching.

After Adem was on the ground and they'd
Transferred the eggs to a cotton-lined basket,
Everyone was able to breathe easily.

The next task was to put the wild dove eggs
Under a domesticated brood pigeon
To hatch them, without his grandmother's knowledge.
Soon enough, she and everyone else would
Know what has happened when the wild squabs would
Be mature enough to exhibit their
Iridescent green and violet purple
Area on their neck amongst white tumblers.

4. The Spirit of the Kalaycik Canyon

He did not want to hear the story of
"The Spirit of the Kalaycik Canyon"
From his grandmother one more time, for he
Had heard it every egg-laying season.

She would begin by saying, "Once upon
A time there was a bright and handsome prince
Who was adored by his father, the king.
The king had many instructors for him
To develop both his mind and body,
So he'd have the skills to take care of himself.
If the prince were kidnapped, he'd be
Able to climb the castle walls to safety.
Being a quick learner and having good
Muscle coordination, in no time
The prince was able to scale any wall.
For further instructions they brought him to
The Kalaycik Canyon to climb its cliffs.

"He was like a spider, as if he were
Attached to the cliffs with invisible
Ropes: he went up and down the cliffs with ease.

"To be presented at his graduation,
The High Priest created a magical
Talisman of a five-pointed gold star.

A string was braided with five distinct
Colors of horsehair, and a red silk pouch.

"While he was descending from his last climb,
A falcon forced the doves into panic,
Which startled the prince who fell to his death.

"A teacher of the prince hid the talisman
In a niche on the cliffs, and it's still there.
The prince was given a proper burial,
Still his soul stayed in the Kalaycik Canyon.

"In his grief, the king held doves liable
For the death of his son. He summoned his
Most skillful archers, and decreed that they
Must exterminate the doves in the Canyon.

"Goddess Kus spread her wings over the doves
Like a thick mist, and the archers could not
See anything beyond their nose to shoot.

"The king's wise man proposed a long-term plan.
He reminded the king that falcons are
The most natural-born hunters of doves.
The wise man said, 'Let us tame the falcons
And turn them loose. They will know what to do.'
When the falconers came to the Kalaycik
Canyon, the Goddess Kus spread her thick mist.
She was not going to allow the bird
Of war to exterminate the bird of peace.
So long as there were cliffs there would be doves.

"I heartily believe that the spirit
Of the prince is benign. He does not mean
To harm the boys; however, he gets lonesome
Each egg-laying season and lures the boys.

"I think that doves are attractive nuisance.
They are the cause of many perished boys:
Sukru Sukuroglu, Tosun Tasoglu…
If you want, I can name them by the dozens.

"I imported my purebred snow-white tumblers
Years ago to breed and to donate them
To any boy who wishes to have them,
Thinking tumblers would be a better choice.

"My tumblers' legs are covered with feathers
That function as an extra pair of wings
To give them a better balance while they're
Turning somersaults high up in the air.

Fledgling tumblers get enthusiastic
And they may lose consciousness while tumbling.
Soon enough they master the proper technique.

"Adem, you are a level-headed boy,
You won't risk your life for a wild dove egg.
If you know any youngster who might be
Tempted to climb the cliffs send him to me.
I'll be glad to give him a pair of tumblers."

5. Back to the Reality

He would wake up and realize that climbing
The cliffs had nothing to do with eggs or
With the Spirit of the Kalaycik Canyon.
It was an unsanctified rite of passage.

Adem's brain would say, "America is
Your canyon and your training is its cliffs.
Do not whine! Either climb or fall and die."

XII.   Can Brainpower Subdue the Feelings?

Once more Adem's willpower would takeover
And he would scold himself, "You're not a bird
That instinctively takes flight when the season
Is right, follows the flock, and at a landing
Place it searches for a proper nesting site.
Act like a man with a mind and mission.
Did you come to America to search
For taller mountains and deeper canyons,
Or to get higher skills and deeper insight?"

He would put his brain to work, and let his
Eyes be soothed by the sea of prairie green.
Still his heart would long for bright Aegean
Blue or light Mediterranean blue.
Then he'd settle for the deep Black Sea blue.

XIII.   Reattachment to the Planet Earth

The city sky offered nothing to watch,
For the stars were hidden above the smog.
When he bought his first car, in search of stars,
He headed to Mt. Taum Sauk, which might have
Been a mountain when she was created
But she must have been shrinking since birth.
Still the skies were clear above the mountain.
As he lay in his sleeping bag, he scanned
The skies and rediscovered the North Star.

Shortly the North Star signaled, "I've shone over
Mt. Olympus, Mt. Ida, Mt. Argaeus.
I've also shone over Homer of Smyrna,
Herodotus of Halicarnassus,
Aesop of Phrygia, Diogenes
Of Sinop, Dede Korkut, Yunus Emre,
Rumi, Karacaoglan, and Seyrani.
I'll continue to shine over the Earth."

At dawn the moon was on the western skies.
And moon's pleasingly plump cheeks were flesh-pink.
When the sun winked at the moon from the east
Without having any hope to touch her,
The moon lost her hale hue; grew gray and waned.

Having seen that, Adem was convinced that
He was reattached to the planet Earth.

XIV. Quick Answers of a Young Man

Youth sow their seeds in the fields of the future.
They may have to wait for the seeds to sprout,
But they have time to wait and see them thrive.

Adem's answers popped without a delay.
For he did not know his identity;
He just displayed his invisible shells.

"I'm a Turk; I was born in Turkiye.
I'm a reservist in the Turkish Airforce,
Also a Korean War veteran.
Sure, I'd love to go back to Turkiye.
I've a fiancée who is a physician.
I have no room in my heart for distrust.
Surely we will be faithful to each other.
All through medical school we were melted
Together and poured into the same mold.
Yes, I have female friends in this country,
But they cannot drive a wedge between us.
All my friends know that I am a stranger
Here who has strong ties to his native land"

XV. The Work Ethics of the Interns of the Fifties

In the fifties the rules were to be obeyed.
The director of the training program
Would tell interns, "You are off duty when
You finish the work-up of your patients."
Though he knew that interns could never finish
Their assignments within regular hours.

In the fifties medical people either
Did not know much about sleep deprivation,
Or they preferred not to talk about it.
Either there were no guidelines regarding
The optimal workload for the training program,
Or they preferred not to talk about them.
Either they did not know about the impacts
Of a heavy workload on the decision
Making capabilities of the interns,
Or they preferred not to talk about them.

The interns of the fifties did not feel
They were being abused by the system.
They thought they were practicing medicine
As their teachers had practiced before them.

They realized they could never control
The inflow of work in medical practice,
Unless they could teach the fetus not to stir,
And people not to have arrhythmia,
Heart attack, or stroke in the dead of night.

For the organized labor a forty-hour

Workweek was an important source of power.
They were making sure that it was enforced.
The interns were using up their quota
Of workweek within a couple of days,
And keep laboring extra days and nights.

The hard work channeled their energies, formed
Their characters, and carried them toward
Their ultimate goals. None of them sustained
Any physical or mental damage.

They were used to seeing each other lying
On the couch, exhausted and fast asleep.
In case one of the slumbering intern was paged,
He could be awakened by the other
Interns who happened to be reading journals.

The edge of competition was too keen.
They were within a pyramid system,
Which had no room at the vertex for all.
Healthy competition has no safe borders:
Jealousy, rivalry and intrigue could
Easily infiltrate into its realm.

XVI. The Coziness of the Nest and the Fear of the Unknown

Adem had been envious more than once.
Before his departure from Ankara,
To bid farewell to his buddies, he went
To the Air Force Base and spotted them at
The officers club. They were playing cards,
Drinking, smoking and enjoying themselves.
They were contented with their lot in life.
He was afraid to risk big, and lose big.
He wanted to tear up his airplane ticket,
His passport and be safe as were his buddies.

When he did arrive in America
He grew envious of the American
Interns for they could take a case history,
Do a physical and write it on the chart,
Thus finish their work-up at the bedside.
He himself had to take notes at the bedside,
Then go to the interns' lounge to refer
To his dictionary and usage books;
To rearrange his notes and turn them into
A salient history and physical.
It would go into the patient's chart only
When he was satisfied with the result.

XVII.   The Cafeteria

The hospital cafeteria functioned
Well as an agora for the young RNs,
Advanced student nurses who already
Earned their caps and capes, interns and residents.
They formed an informal clique without rules.
Each one was both a shopper and a browser
According to his/her inclination.

The business was low keyed and low pressured.
They knew how to take each other's pulse
From the level of each other's emotions,
And take each other's temperature from
The degree of warmth of each other's smiles,
Then make a diagnosis if the other
One was in the mood for after-hours business.

The cafeteria also functioned
As an unsanctified sanctuary.
Its smoky air was less oppressive than
The air of conference rooms and libraries,
For there they had control over their time.
If they were to receive a routine call,
They could finish their coffee without feeling
As if they were neglecting their duties.
They'd tell others, "Eat slowly and chew well."
But they ate fast knowing that at any
Second an emergency might happen.

To foster friendship, the cafeteria
Was at its best soon after nine at night.

By then most of the crowd would have gone home;
Just the core crew would have been left behind.
The night shift had a cordial interaction.

XVIII.　Ann McCann

On that night, quiet was the cafeteria.
Only a few tables were occupied,
And a young nurse was sitting all alone.
Adem joined her without introducing
Himself as if he had known her before.
She did most of the talking, and he listened.
"My name is Ann McCann. I recently
Moved from Seattle to sunny St. Louis.
I'm already missing the cleansing rain.
This evening is my first shift at this place."
As her vibrant words were reaching his brain,
They were echoing a most pleasing sound.

When she was returning to her station,
He observed her measured movements and said,
"A fine figure and an enchanting voice."
As if his mind were an echo chamber,
Ann's voice echoed in it all through the night.
He scolded himself, "It must be merely
Déjà vu, or you are going crazy.
What makes you think you've known her all along?"

1. Remembering Queen Haseki Hospital

Then his mind shifted to the Queen Haseki
Hospital, which was founded for women.
Dr. Kozanoglu would be lecturing,
And as usual he would be larding
His lecture with anecdotes, "This hospital
Is dedicated for beauty herself.

The Queen decreed, 'Any lady may be
Eligible for free care if she has
Husnu endam and Husnu Sada.'"
Then he would pause and the students would say,
"We don't understand your Ottoman Turkish.
Hodja, please repeat it in modern Turkish."
Then he would reword, "A lady must have
A fine figure and an enchanting voice."

He would leave the classroom with the head nurse.
By the time they'd reached the hallway, interns
And residents would complete the entourage.

The students would act as a restive horde,
And shoot arrows of questions from all sides.
"Hodja, don't you think that the Queen was vain?
How could she ask that a patient must have
A fine figure and an enchanting voice.
Shall we deny care for a shrill fat shrew?"
He would answer, "All my days I have never
Seen any ugliness or heard disharmony.
Look and see: beauty is all around you.
Hark and hear: music is all around you."

2. I Have Learned to See Beauty All Around

The next day Adem took his coffee break
Early and occupied the same table.
Soon after Ann glided in and joined him.
That evening he was not only hearing
The mesmerizing music of her voice,
But also beholding the beauty all
Around him: dancing bright eyes, long eyelashes,
Curling of lips while vowels and consonants
Were pronounced, and the rhythmic body language.
In his mind he was reporting to
Dr. Kozanoglu, "Yes, Dear Hodja,
I've learned to see the beauty all around.
I've learned to hear the music all around."

Then he'd muse about what the Muses said,
"We know how to speak false things that seem true,
But we know, when we will, to tell true things."

His restless mind still would be asking questions,
"Am I beholding and hearing true things?"

3. Getting Closer Without Crossing the Line

Sharing their breaks became a ritual.
They learned how to dive deep into the ocean
Of emotions without making a ripple.

He had applied the same techniques on Nuran,
And without resorting to the flowery
Language of lovers, he had been able
To dive deeper into the depths of love.

Ann would bubble over when she would talk
About the Cascade Mountains, and they would
Sound young and fiery, though unlike the old
Mountains with spent volcanoes that he knew,
About the San Juan Islands, and they would
Sound rainy and lush, though unlike the warm
And sunbaked ancient islands that he knew,
About the Pacific Ocean, and it
Would sound fathomless, though unlike the tepid,
Calm and friendly inland seas that he knew.
Yet they were missing the same kind of things,
And were enjoying the same kind of things.

After their visits he would be perplexed
By questions for which he had no answers.
He would ask, "What is the color of Ann's eyes?"
He would answer, "It is Aegean blue."
Then he would change his mind, "Yes, I know now.
It is a hue of a high meadow green."

His mind would drift back to Halicarnassus
To find a place where he could not be fooled
By the outward appearances of things.
However, he had the same problem with
The true color of all those pristine coves.
They would look blue now, then they would grow green.

In time, they made Angilo's Nightclub
Their haunt for their quick visits after work.
Their entertainment remained table talk.
Adem would read Nuran's recent letter,
And tell what they'd talked about on the phone.
She would talk about, Brian, her husband.
It was not the theme of the dialogue
That was important, but the flow of it,
And the silent moments they spent together.

Ann loved to dance, and she was good at it.
She danced as if she had no skeletal
Frame to diminish her rhythmicity.

She could have made an entrancing priestess.
After casting her spell over the labor
Weary worshipers with her rhythmic dancing,
She would promise them Elysian Fields,
And they would have sincerely believed her,
For they would think that the goddess of heaven
Was the one who was speaking through her priestess.

XIX. The Single Fathers, Teenagers and Policemen of the Fifties

In the fifties there were no paramedics
As "Emergency Medical Technicians."
The policemen and firemen of the fifties
Acted as today's licensed technicians.

In the emergency room, the house staff
And policemen worked next to each other.
When the shooting and stabbing victims came,
Their legal and social plights followed them.
The policemen were there to spread a thin
Layer of calmness over the chaos.

1. Erden Eroglu and Beyazit Square

To have an accurate understanding
Of the psychology of American
Policemen, Adem's mind recalled his
Policeman roommate, Erden Eroglu.
He was a few years older than Adem,
And both of them came from the same province.
They had shared an apartment for a couple
Of years in the neighborhood of Beyazit
Square in Istanbul, a business district,
Not suited for families with children,
But an advantageous location for
A student and a rookie policeman.

Beyazit Square provided everything
That Adem hoped to have: The library
Of Beyazit Mosque was open year-round
For him to use it as a study hall,
And the University of Istanbul
Was there to obtain his M.D. degree.

2. Spirit of the River

In those days it looked as if Adem were
Driven by the lure of his future goals.
Though he was living his life according
To his grandmother's "Spirit of the River."
She would finish her tale by saying, "Life
Is like a river. Now it's calm and calming,
Then it turns turbulent and threatening.
Nevertheless, it can't afford to stop.
To be a river, that river must flow,
And must replenish itself drop by drop.

"Adem, you were born with the best of gifts:
A brilliant mind and a healthy body.
You are sensible enough to make use
Of your gifts, which will lead you to your goals.
However, my promising prediction
Has nothing to do with real happiness.

"Our lives are made of drops of passing moments.
Once they pass by, they will never return.
To draw out joy from each passing moment,
Let your eyes see the grace in everything:
Cherish every snowflake before it melts;
During a hot summer day when the rain
Comes down, let its drops filter through your hair.
Smell the fragrance flowing from sprinkled fields.
After the rain, scan the hues of the rainbow
Without going to the end of the rainbow.

As you sit under a weeping willow
Let its dewy leaflets fondle your face.
Life is meant to be lived not to be won."

3. Beyazit Mosque

Historically Beyazit Mosque was
The second royal mosque in Istanbul.
It turned into the first surviving one,
When the first built Mosque of Fatih was burned.
Adem did not have to go out of his
Way to see the Mosque. It'd be there to greet
Him whenever he passed over the square.

4. Open-air Coffeehouse and Neyzen.

At the south side of the Mosque an open-air
Coffeehouse was located, which was shaded
By enormous ancient sycamore trees.
Janizaries used to frequent that place.
During the last couple of centuries,
It's been haunted by the poets and pundits.
In the late forties, satirist poet
And flautist Neyzen was its famous guest.

Neyzen symbolized living history,
For Adem and other college students.
He was born during the turbulent years
Of the declining Ottoman Empire,
The last quarter of the nineteenth century.
Young Turks were determined to abolish
The monarchy and resolved to establish
A constitutional form of government.

Neyzen joined Young Turks and as they had done,
He left the empire, to get away from

The censure of the royal policemen,
And to work freely in foreign countries.
He returned when freedom was obtained.

He saw the loss of the Balkan countries,
The collapse of the Great Turkish Empire
Due to World War I, the worst fate yet,
The occupation of the Motherland;
The liberation war and finally
The birth of the Republic of Turkiye.

For flute lovers he was the Pied Piper.
The concert halls tried but failed to book him.
He might or might not show for a performance.
Istanbulians were not discouraged.
They knew, he'd perform when he was inspired.

Whenever Neyzen went to a nightclub,
The word would get around, and music lovers
Would pack that establishment hoping that
Night might be their lucky night to receive
The gift of music from the master flautist.

All through his life, he lived on the line that
Divides sanity from insanity.
He used alcohol and other drugs, either
To grow insane or to gain his sanity.

He never learned how to manage money.
He gave a concert at King Resat's palace.
He was given a silk purse of gold coins.
On his way home, he noticed the wagons
Of Turkish refugees from the Balkans.
He stopped and dealt out gold coins among them.
By the time his companion could say, "Save
A piece for yourself," the last piece was gone.

According to the standards of people,
He was leading a life of poverty.
He himself said, "I am the richest man

In Istanbul, for all doors in the city
Open wide for me and I am welcomed."

5. Courtyard of the Beyazit Mosque

When Adem passed through the square, he could not
Go by without noticing the Mosque's courtyard:
A peristyle of twenty ancient columns—
Porphyry, verd antique and rare granite—
Formed an arcade picked out by alternating
Red-and-white or black-and-white voussoir and
A portico covered by twenty-four domes.
Over the centuries those stones had been
Damaged by age or repeated earthquakes,
And the cracked and crumbled, older stones had
Been replaced with new ones except the hue
Of the colors could not be closely matched.
That appearance proved that the Mosque was ancient.

6. Forum of Theodosius

When Adem wandered toward the south side
Of Beyazit Square and saw the remnants
Of the Forum of Theodosius,
He'd realize that at the ancient Square
What looked old was new in comparison
To the next structure which was even older.

7. The University of Istanbul

Whenever Adem passed through the Portal
Of The University of Istanbul,
And walked through the long greens and old sycamore
Trees and arrived at the stately main buildings,
He was in a lately reorganized
University with German professors,
Or was it a pilgrimage to the Seat

Of the power, for the same buildings once
Was the Ottoman Defense Ministry.

On the campus there stood a two-hundred—
Foot-tall fire watchtower of white marble.
When he climbed to its top, Adem marveled
At Istanbul, the Sea of Marmara,
The Golden Horn, and the Bosphorus as
Many a mortal had done before him.

8. The Beauty of the Location of Istanbul

The ancient Greeks were bewitched by the native
Beauty of the location of Istanbul.
They founded the city of Byzantium,
Six centuries before the birth of Jesus.
Eight centuries later the Romans fell
Under its spell; they rebuilt it as their
Capital and named it Constantinople.
It reigned as the great Eastern European
Imperial Capital for sixteen
Centuries safe and sound behind its walls.
When the Turks acquired that exquisite Jewel,
They placed it on the crown of their empire.

9. The Sea of Marmara

The beauty of the Sea of Marmara
Alone was enough to satisfy Adem.
It had many moods to thrill anyone:
Most of the time playful and pacific,
Suddenly, powerful and perilous.

10. Sahaflar Carsisi

Sahaflar Carsisi, "The Old Book Bazaar,"
Was located next to the Mosque's courtyard.

A picturesque and vivacious market
In whose shops, book lovers could find secondhand
Books and new editions in any language.

One-of-a-kind manuscripts and handwritten and
Hand-illustrated books kept in vaults:
Although shopkeepers would gladly display
Them for anybody interested
To pass the word of their existence.

11. The Grand Bazaar

The Grand Bazaar spread out next to the Mosque.
It was a city in a larger city.
On first entering, the great market looked
A bewildering maze to Adem.
Before long, he learned the grid-like arrangements
Of its streets and squares, and used them as shortcuts
As he got around the old Istanbul.

Adem felt at home in the Grand Bazaar,
When he could pass those restaurants with bright
Neon lights, which would cater to the tourists,
And find the small restaurants known only
By the locals for its delicious dishes.

Such a unique restaurant was managed
By a cranky Ottoman palace cook.
Adem and Nuran frequented that place.
After savoring the food, at times they
Would tease the cook, "If you redecorate
Your restaurant you'd have a booming business."
The Cook, "I've more business than I can handle.
Get out of my restaurant. Don't come back."
Some other time, they'd say, "You're a master chef,
But today your food tasted rather bland."
The Cook, "Get out of my restaurant; come
Back when you acquire a taste for the fine
Food that pleased the palates of kings and queens."

12. Neighborhood of Adem and Erden

Adem and Erden roomed in a small building.
On the first floor there was a tailor shop,
On the second a lawyer and his staff,
On the third a dentist and his apartment,
On the fourth two residential units.
In one of them, Adem and Erden lived,
And in the other lived Mr. and Mrs.
Kavadias and their son Kosta.

Some time ago the Kavadias couple
Moved to Istanbul from Anatolia.
To develop better business connections,
Mr. Kavadias had to learn Greek.
Mrs. Kavadias was contented
To live without learning a word of Greek.
She kept reading her Bible in Turkish.
Their son, Kosta, was fluent in both tongues,
Which served him well. He'd pose as a Greek with
Greek girls and as a Turk with Turkish girls.

Kosta was about the same age as Adem.
He owned and ran his one-man tailor shop.
He'd visit and dine with Adem and Erden.
He must have savored the companionship,
For the meals they shared were merely meager.

Sometimes Mrs. Kavadias would fix
The best meals and bring them to Adem's place.
After setting the table, she would leave
To let Adem, Erden and Kosta savor
The banquet without being monitored.

She was a plain Anatolian mother
Who wore no makeup. One could discover
A hint of eyeliner, which looked natural.
Her black hair was pulled back to form a bun.
She had no middle age bulges or wrinkles.
That caring lady was never prying

Or preachy; still on proper occasions
She would quote a verse or two from the Bible.

Adem and Erden had little contact
With the sly dentist and his windy wife.
They referred to the wife as Babushka,
Since they were Russian-Turkish immigrants.

Adem saw Babushka just in the hallway.
Each time she'd tell that she and her husband
Were undercover agents in the Turkish
Secret Service. They operated as
Advisors regarding to Russian Affairs.
Adem and Erden would sketch spying plots.
Babushka would be one of their blabbering
Characters who would quickly spill the beans.
In each plot she'd be the butt of their jokes.

13. Personality of Erden

Erden had a split personality.
When he put on his police uniform
And wore his gun belt, he metamorphosed
And grew taller and heavier than himself.
He also transformed psychologically,
And became another man who could not
Trust anybody walking on this Earth.
He thought that everyone was capable
Of committing an unexpected crime.
He had to keep his guard up at all times.

When he finished his shift and took his
Uniform off, put his gun in a drawer
And slipped into his civilian clothes,
He lost his ready to take-charge mind-set.
His psyche reclaimed its healthy condition.
Once more he grew friendly and openhearted.

Erden kept their apartment immaculate,
Prepared their breakfast and packed Adem's lunch.
When Adem would say, "Erden, when I come
Back from school, I see that all chores are done,
And there is nothing left for me to do.
I like it, though I feel like a freeloader.
Please make a list of chores that I should do."

Erden would answer with a raucous voice
As if he were commanding a halt, "Adem,
If you like to nest in this dump, clean it.
If you like to fly away as soon as
You can, then let me be the housekeeper.
It is given that my work is demanding.
The law must be enforced by somebody until
Men evolve to a level where they'll need
No policeman, no judge and no jury.

"At this phase of our lives, I work eight hours.
Whereas you have to burn the midnight oil
Before your midterm and final exams.
What I do for you is a gift. Take it."

Adem lifted his head, focused his bright
Eyes on Erden, swept his one big brown curl
Sideways, which was dangling down on his forehead
Just like a male mallard's curled tail coverts,
Gave a grateful smile to honor Erden's
Gift without uttering a single word.

14. Adem's Mind Shifted Back to the U.S

When the American policemen talked
About high crime rate in the city:
"There was no safe neighborhood or safe house;
Even the policemen's family members
Can be victimized by prowling perverts;
Even their teenage daughters can be raped;
And they couldn't be there to protect them."

Adem understood them. These men were not
A bunch of paranoid schizophrenics.
Actually, they were behaving according
To the realities of their profession.

Frank Johnson was one of the policemen
Who was employed as a full-time deputy
In the St. Louis County Sheriff Department,
And moonlighted as a hospital police.
As a single parent, he was raising
His two spirited sons all by himself.

At the police academy, Frank reigned
As the heavyweight boxing champion.
He kept his natural heavyweight figure
With broad shoulders, firm muscles and small hips.
He would not allow himself to puff up:
No bulging belly, no flabby muscles.
He was a quiet man until the topic
Of conversation was shifted to his
Sons' and hunting dogs' daily activities.

Frank would say, "I have more respect
For foreign interns than Americans.
Foreign ones come from faraway countries;
They learn the language in no time and flourish
While the American interns make it
In their country without enduring hardship."

Frank and Adem fostered a lasting friendship.
They even had a physical resemblance,
Except Adem was a natural light
Heavyweight and had the speed of that class.

Whether young men were the best friends or not,
They'd find a way to test each other's strength.
Arm-wrestling was an easy way to do it.
Adem was the winner each time they tried.
At last Frank was convinced that he was beaten
Fair and square, and it was not a stroke of luck.

Seeing that, he became the self-appointed
Manager of Adem and promoted
Arm-wrestling matches, and took pleasure when
His champion defeated his big buddies.

Frank's sons were handsome, full of energy,
And they were also in style with their ducktails.
Eric, fourteen, was reserved and a smoker.
John, nine, was a friendly and gifted child.

After a sport event they stopped at Adem's.
John shuffled the records and found his trophy.
He was flagging one of Elvis Presley's
Records and saying, "See, dad, a grown-up
Doctor can be an Elvis Presley fan.
I'm gonna tell my teacher that there is
Nothing wrong with being an Elvis Fan."

15. Ann's Comments

The next day Adem told Ann, he was pleased
By having the company of Frank's sons,
Though he did not approve of the older
Son being a seasoned smoker at fourteen.
"Had I smoked at his age, I could not have
Found a hole to hide in, for every old
Man or woman in my town would've stopped me
And lectured me about the evils of smoking,
Even though they themselves might be smoking."

Ann said, "Your mind can analyze past events,
And try to project them upon the future.
When you witness a happenstance pertaining
To childhood experiences, your mind
Goes back to where you were a child to find
Similar incidents to solve the puzzle.
It's perplexing that human experiences
Happen under unique circumstances,
And its parts are not interchangeable.

"Do you appreciate Negro Music?"
"Yes Ma'am. I love their hoarse and haunting sound
And their lively beat." "You are not alone.
Lots of people derive pleasure from it,
Though they do not care to acknowledge it.
For the taste of the new generation,
Today's soft music is too insipid.
For a long time, white kids have been buying
The discs of Black musicians and singers.

"When white kids heard the rhythm and blues coming
From the lips of a young white man with blue
Eyes and gyrating hips they fell for it.

"Young girls who were ready to fall in love
For the first time found Elvis ready-made.
Elvis is a symbol of a cultural
Mass movement, but not the founder of it.
He is riding over the waves that are
Caused by the influence of Black culture.

"The keepers of the tradition will fight
To keep the status quo. How can they ever
Win against the recently acquired taste
Of youth when it satisfies their sexual
Fantasies as well as musical needs?
How can they hush their transistor radios?

"Frank belongs to a new generation
Of the Good-Old-American-Boys Club.
These men are both courageous and credulous.
They are daring to raise a family
Without having prior experience.

"Frank is holding so many jobs to offer
His sons more material objects than
He received as a post-depression child,
While he is denying his sons the values
That he himself received during his childhood:

The security of a whole corporate
Family life that protected him from
The ill effects of outside forces till
He himself developed his own taproots:
A mother to nurture him and a father
With strong hands to steer him to the straight path.

"Frank is neither fathering nor guiding
His sons; he is merely palling with them.
When he sees his son's smoking, he is not
Taking a stand as his father would have
Taken and say, 'Boy! Stop this nonsense now!
One addiction invites another one!'

"Frank is acting as the promiscuous
Parents of nowadays. He is saying,
'Pal! You know smoking is hazardous for
Your well-being. Why don't you choose to quit?'

"The freedom of choice is a heavy load
To carry on the back of a teenager.
Everybody knows it well; unless there
Is a protective screen around a candle,
A moth will always choose to burn itself."

XX.   Give-and-Take

During the middle of his internship,
Adem was summoned to personnel office,
And informed that he had a one time offer
To interchange his exchange student visa
With a permanent resident visa.
He took the forms to think about the offer.

1. Adem's Mind Returned to Kayseri

A small street sign read, *Ademoglu Street.*
Down the road he passed *Ademoglu Mosque.*
He kept walking a few blocks more and pulled
A huge key from his pocket to open
The heavily studded main entrance doors,
Then passed through the house and entered the garden.
He followed the pathway, which was paved with
Polished tuff, toward the sycamore tree.
Its trunk was leaning over the retainer
Walls around the pond. He climbed up and straddled
The place where the branches formed a saddle.
He felt like a kid: singing, and the storks
On the chimney were providing the music.

Nothing had changed. When he was a youngster
He thought that the sycamore tree was too
Ancient then, and it was too ancient now.
The granite foundation of the old house
Was too gray then, and it was too gray now.

He then paid a visit to the family graveyard.
He could not decipher the inscriptions
On the tombstones, for they were carved in old
Turkish scripts, although he knew by heart,
Each stone which belonged to each ancestor.
He cleaned the marbles, being careful not
To step over the graves; he sat on the ground,
And prayed for the souls of his ancestors.

2. Adem's Mind Was with Nuran

He then was with Nuran, and they were rushing
Through the campus of the medical school,
And then through the streets of Old Istanbul.

He was not interested in knowing
How many generations of lovers
Had passed through the same narrow streets to polish
The cobblestones of that romantic city.
He had no desire to hear the echoes
Of their love songs, nor did he care to know
Whether their loves had grown sweet or turned sour.

He was absorbed by the love of Nuran.
It was in his blood and circulating
All through his systems to nourish his being.
He was dropping a few steps behind her
To form a single file to let her flow
Freely through the narrow and uneven
Sidewalks, and to behold her balanced steps,
Shapely legs, fine shiny hair which was flying
Off her neck and giving him a quick peek
Of her snow-white skin. Then she was slowing,
Turning her head, giving a winsome wink,
Saying, "Come on! Don't fall too far behind."

As he was filling out the immigration
Papers, Nuran's voice was echoing in
His mind, "Come on! Don't fall too far behind."

He opted not to change his visa status.
For the echoes of pleasant voices were
Hoping to lure him back to his homeland.

3. Give-and-Take American-Style

That evening he told Ann what had happened
And said, "*This is a Generosity—*
American-Style." Ann said, "I'd restate
It as, '*Give-and-Take American-Style*.'"

"We have been involved in French Indochina
Even prior to the Korean War.
Slowly Vietminhs phlebotomized France.
They were ready to end their long lasting
Colonial war, and America
Was planning to step in for a good cause?
'To terminate the spread of communism.'

"Every bloody war must have an appealing
Cause for the people to sacrifice themselves.
They have now '*The domino theory*:
When the first one is knocked, the last one falls.'

"John Foster Dulles is running around
The world to find nations to side with us.
Even if he were to succeed in finding
Participating nations, it will not
Be of help for the American boys.

"You have seen what happened in Korea.
It was a joint effort; still brooks of blood
Was shed by the American soldiers.
They are saying, 'We have but two choices:
To stop the communists in their own countries,
Or fight them on American mainland.'
Why can't we have a third choice, and choose not
To fight with any nation sharing the Earth.

"We can't manufacture physicians just
Like war machinery for the armed forces.
Why not tap the pool of foreign physicians?
Give them legal status and then draft them.
Those who are eager to receive favors
Must return the favor some other way.

"How about my brothers and my husband?
When the war starts, will they have any choice?
To go or not to go? To kill or not
To kill? To be killed or not to be killed?

"I lost an uncle during World War II,
And another one returned from Korea,
However, he is more dead than alive.
He is wasting his life away either
In a drunk tank or in a rehab unit
Of a VA Hospital to recover
Enough to repeat the vicious cycle."

Adem said to himself, "Oh my goodness,
Am I now discovering the bitter side
Of Miss American Pie, or is she
Like Cassandra who can foretell the future,
However, nobody will believe her?"

The foreign physicians who accepted
The US Permanent Residency
Visa were in military uniforms
By the end of their internship program.

XXI.   The Midterm Crises

Adem was happy to receive his contract
For the next year's residency program.
Before long interns were whispering,
"The residency contracts are not binding."
He said, "If these people won't honor their
Signature, surely, they won't keep their word.
Do not waste your breath by talking with them.
You find a residency somewhere else
And tell them, sorry, I can't work with you!"
But he knew his options were limited.

He felt as if he were treading water
In an ocean among the weighty sharks
While they were feeding on small fish like himself.

1. Adem Solicited Nuran's Help

He called Nuran and said, "Now I am standing
Where the river forks, and I must decide
Whether to take the west fork or the east;
Whether to keep swimming against the side
Currents to reach my goal without being
Capsized, and carried away from Turkiye
And you by the main stream of America,
Or to return to the University
Of Istanbul and start from the beginning."

Nuran said, "To speed the process, I can
Get the application forms and send them.
Please fill them out and mail them back to me.

I'll give them to the proper authorities,
And we will find a position for you."

2. 'Dear Son' Letter

He called his parents and gave them the news.
They did not sound happy about his plan.
They said, "We will write and let you know how
We feel about this recent development."
Within a week a 'Dear Son' letter came.

"Love and greetings: Love reveals herself with
Thousands of phases. Each one of her phase
Is unlike the other one, for each phase
Surpasses the next one in charm and grace.

"When we see her first phase, we fix our eyes
On that phase for we are quite contented.
When life forces twist our heads and when we
Recover from the effect of that jolt,
Then do our eyes behold her other phases?
Happy are the ones who see love's first phase.
Blessed are the ones who see love's many phases.

"When we say, We love both you and Nuran,
Our word has an unfathomable depth.
When we held you in our arms as a newborn,
It cured our tunnel vision and our eyes
Beheld many phases of love at once.
The concept of responsibility
Gained a new meaning since you were a gift
For us to take care of temporarily,
And then turn you loose to take care of yourself.

"We have shown you just the main roads of life.
We said, 'Be strong.' You have been strong so long.
Thus being strong brought you where you are now.
To go further in life you must discover
That every day life is an interaction

Between you and the world all around you,
Where there are forces that one can't control.
Now it is time for you to learn to bend
In front of the fierce winds just like a reed.

"Thus far you have seen the first phase of love.
Are you willing to continue to love
Each other in order to see and cherish
All other phases of love together?

"Remember, we did not want you to leave
Your country, or your fiancée behind.
Now we must say, 'Stay in America
Until you materialize your goals.'

"Here folks might say, 'Ademoglu's son has
No grits or guts. He ran back home, for he
Could not pass muster in America.'
With this we can cope; still we are concerned
That Nuran is acting as your mentor.
Therefore we are afraid that your feelings
Of gratitude toward her will grow sour.
Then they will turn into indebtedness.
Can you cope with those kinds of lame feelings?
Love can thrive under adverse conditions,
But she can't bloom by breathing borrowed air.

"Don't fool yourself; you're not there to gain ground.
But you are there to not just be a junior
Colleague of Nuran here in Turkiye.
We have told you that in the School of Life
People are not graded on the same subject.
They succeed or fail in their chosen fields.
While you were paying your debt to your country,
Nuran advanced in the medical field.
You are both winners; but can you nurture
Love and let her thrive by being winners?

"You have reason to be proud of each other;
Yet love knows no pride. You try to sustain

Your love with a 'win-win' relationship.
But love risks more and more to play the game.
The contest is a wedge between the lovers.

"If you must return, come back home without
Making any arrangement through Nuran.
Lose time. Fall further behind, but determine
Your own future with your own volition
To center your love on the same footing.
You are not a chick who can be cozy
Under the warm wings of a brooding hen."

XXII.   The Decision by Default

Adem received a large envelope from
The University of Istanbul.
But he did not open it, for he was
Not ready to decide, or to take action.

He would not open his personal letters,
Nor would he receive his off-duty calls.
While working, he'd lift the receiver gently,
If it were a duty-related call,
He'd perk up and run to where he was needed.

One midnight the operator said, "Doctor,
Your fiancée is on the line." Adem
Was not ready to say, 'Yes, Dear, I will
Return to Istanbul, or I will finish
The rest of my training in America.'

He began to visit as lovers do.
But Nuran pressed for a definite answer.
"Have you filled out the forms and mailed them back?"
Then he was forced to say, "I'd like to finish
My residency in America."

She continued with endearments of lovers:
She neither used her gift of persuasion
Nor did she accuse him of using her…
Not a word about him being unsettled
To let her lose her credibility,
Not a word, such as, 'how long must I wait?'
But he sensed that the bond of love was broken
Without any audible, snapping sound.

His past and future were split into two.
At that time, Adem did not care to know
As to what might be in store in the future.
He fixed his mind into the happy segments
Of his past where Nuran was in his life.

Everything that had happened while they were
Basking in their togetherness was there:
Unembellished, undisturbed and unchanged,
As if they were painstakingly painted,
In vivid colors, by a master painter.
No details were neglected or left out.

Their very first and last kiss were still fresh,
Though bygone events were just like silk flowers,
Pinned on the changeless canvas of the past,
Without promising any future blossoms.

XXIII. What Becomes of a Broken Love?

What happens to the broken love of lovers?
Does it grow wings to soar into the heavens?
Does it wear away and turn into dust?
Does it combust and consume itself without
Giving light or without leaving any ashes?

What do young lovers with their broken love?
Do they tear it down and toss out its parts?
Do they use its parts to build a new love?
Do they exhale it like stale breath of air—
Dispersing it into the atmosphere?
Do they bury it under their subconscious
By daylight, and bring it to life by night?
After ejecting it out of their hearts,
Do they remove its invisible scars?
Do they say love is but an illusion?
Or do they say it felt good while it lasted!

XXIV. Was it an Expression of Love?

Adem went to the oncology ward
To see Ms. Jones. She was a ruined temple,
Yet the altar was still perceptible.
He envisioned her as she might have looked
When she was a young and healthy woman.

He gave normal turgor to her slack skin,
And plumped her cells to get rid of her wrinkles,
Then removed her senile keratoses,
Covered her vitiligo spots with pigment,
And let her skin shine as smooth ebony.

He straightened her kyphotic spinal column,
Put on the right amount of supple muscles
And supportive subcutaneous tissues,
And gave her back her fleshy curvaceousness.

He then turned her gray hair back to raven,
Gave her a straight set of healthy white teeth,
Filled in her hollow cheeks back to their wholeness,
And gave her back her voluptuous lips,
Then slightly parted them with a warm smile,
Filled in her sunken orbs, brightened her eyes,
And let them sparkle with the spark of life.

When he'd rebuilt a young image for her,
He said to himself, "When she was emitting
Energy owing to health and beauty,
Someone must have loved her. Where is he now?"

Adem left the ward. Down the hall, he noticed
An elderly gentleman who was leaning
On his cane with his right hand to support
His weight, and holding a rose in his left,
And trying to figure out the room numbers.

Behind his thick glasses his eyes appeared
Magnified and distorted. They looked like
A pair of unpolished and mottled marbles.

Adem asked if could help. The man answered,
With a broad smile that beamed warmth into hearts,
And spread goodwill without mouthing a word.
"Please lead me to the room 613 C.
I'd like to visit my wife, Mrs. Jones."

When she heard her husband's shuffling footsteps,
She quickened to muster up enough strength
To run her fingers through her matted hair,
Wiped up the cold sweat from her face and neck,
Smeared some lipstick to moisten her dry lips,
Rubbed some kind of perfume behind her ears,
And covered her grimace with a faint smile.
And then two pairs of dry lips gently kissed.

That simple kiss was etched on Adem's brain.
It became a permanent background set.
He saw that scene of kiss behind all things.

What it meant? Was it an apology?
For a long-forgotten lovers' quarrel?
A ghost of wet kisses of yesteryears?
A reward for an attained achievement?
A payment for a debt owed long ago?
Or an expression of a lifelong love?

XXV.   Self Isolation

Adem isolated himself within
The realm of work not to allow himself
Any spare time to cherish his new friends.

He was applying to second rate places
To get an appointment for the next year.
He was not sure whether he was coming
Out of his shell, or boring into it.

While he was rushing through the corridors
Of the hospital; he was stopped by Ann.
"Hi stranger! You have been shunning your friends.
Tonight you may meet me at Angilo's.
There you will have the right to defend yourself."

That night at Angilo's, he felt awkward.
He did not know how to act; what to say,
For the foundation of their relationship
Was no longer on an equal footing.
Here was a woman who could lose her marriage,
While he was free and had nothing to lose.

To put him at ease, Ann did the talking:
No prying, no questioning, just chatting.
Then he loosened up, "I am trying
To shun no one else except my own self,
Yet it is not working, for wherever
I go, whatever I do, I'm with myself.

"Mainly, I did not want to talk with you,
For I did not know what I ought to say.

Since you are my echo and my mirror,
I shunned you, for you will echo how I
Might sound, and might reflect how I will look.
I was not ready to hear the echoes
Of my empty heart or to see my face.

"I still love Nuran, although in the future,
We have to journey on parallel paths.
One might think, doing your own thing is easy;
One is free to succeed or free to fail,
But where is the yardstick to measure it?
I will have to learn, all over again,
To journey on a new path: step by step,
Stopping to see if I'm on the right course.

"I think I took one wrong step already.
For years, I have been keeping my Turkish
Poetry book nearby to comfort me.
I used to read it to quicken my feelings.
After our separation, I read it
Once more hoping that it might heighten
My spirits, and put me in touch with life.
Last time poems sounded as if they were
Empty and hollow words. I burned them all."

When they began to dance, he was consciously
Inspecting himself as to what was proper.
He was aware of the minor details,
And was analyzing his every movement.
"Am I holding her tight as lovers do?
Am I getting too close to her body?"
It was no longer lighthearted enjoyment.

His mind went back to the Marmaris Coast.
During his summer recess, he was working
As a sponge diver and the temptation
To dive deep and deeper into the waters
Of the Aegean Sea was always there,
Not to get the prize sponge to make more money,
But to prove the point that a highlander

Can be as agile under the heavy
Weight of the salty seawaters as he
Could be under the thin air of the highlands.
Then he must have known instinctively how
Deep to dive, and where to stop before drowning.

Sometimes it is more exciting to sail
On a calm sea, for only then can one
Hear the soft music of the gentle waves,
And see the color displays of the sea.

And now, while dancing, he was not willing
To churn the feelings they were sailing on.

XXVI.   The Burial of the Memories

Ann brought Adem to the present by saying,
"You lost an object of love, but never
The love itself, which will accumulate
Drop by drop and will overflow its channel.
For that to happen, you must free yourself
From articles that symbolize your love.
Those souvenirs have a way growing
Into icons, and turning the keepers
Of the icons into iconolaters.

"I'd like you to find all those big or small
Souvenirs that might remind you of Nuran,
And amass them. I will put them to rest."

When Ann came to conduct the ritual,
She laid down her scissors, tapes, wrapping papers,
Ribbons, and boxes next to the souvenirs.
While she was sorting out the sacks of love
Letters, photographs and other trinkets,
She was encouraging Adem to tell
Little tales that were attached to each item,
And listening as if they were important.

Ann put them in envelopes and boxes,
And sealed them. Then she fitted them into
A larger box, taped it shut, and handed
The box back to Adem for safekeeping.

He was consoled, for a priestess had given
A burial with a solemn service
To the remains of his still memories.

XXVII.   Fairness-American-Style

Adem was attending a conference.
The last lecturer was Dr. Dalton,
The Director of the Training Program.
From the beginning Dr. Dalton's eyes
Were focused on Adem, which made him tense.
Adem shifted his weight, looked sideways,
Down to the floor and up to the ceiling,
Still he could not escape from the piercing
Gaze of his teacher. When the conference
Was over, he darted towards the door,
But he was stopped by Dr. Dalton's voice.
The teacher was trying to be kind-hearted;
Still his seriousness was obvious.

As they walked, Dr. Dalton was asking,
"Did you find the lecture interesting?"
"Yes, Sir I did." "Do you have any question?"
"No, Sir, you covered your topic thoroughly."

When they reached the door of the interns' lounge,
Adem entered just like a scared rabbit
Darts into the safety of its burrow.
He found no safety there, for Dr. Dalton
Had followed him and plopped down next to him.
Adem felt as if someone was pursuing
Him for a crime that he had not committed.

"Do you mind if I ask a few questions?"
"No, Sir. Please do." Dr. Dalton began
To quiz him by giving case histories,
And asking Adem how he'd manage them.

As they discussed these academic cases,
Dr. Dalton's piercing gaze grew softer.
They began to treat each other as colleagues.
Then the quiz turned into a pastime of
'If that should happen, what do you do next?'

When the subject matter came to cortisone,
Adem put down the biochemical
Formula of the primary compound.
Then he attached to it a short side chain,
Created a new compound and explained
Its advantages and disadvantages
By comparing with the mother compound.
He continued to rearrange the side
Chains to name other related compounds.

Adem was having fun with his formulas
Like a child playing with his blocks and saying,
'See, Dad, what I can do now?' When he finished
Playing with his side chains, Dr. Dalton said,
"The day you complete your internship is
The day you will start your residency."

He told Ann what has happened and added,
"I call this, *Fairness-American-Style*"

XXVIII. The Social Problems

Social problems do not follow the patients
To the hospitals, but they lead them there.
In turn, medical problems and contagious
Plagues change the moral values of people.

Every social ill is conceived and brought
Forth and cared for by each society.
To diagnose any social illness,
One must be part of that society.

Adem was not well prepared to handle
The problems of pregnant, but unwed women.
When he faced one of them, he would expect
To see a husband with her who is ready
To take responsibility for raising
A child in a nurturing environment.

Adem was called to deliver a baby.
The nurse was presenting the medical
History of the parturient mother:
"This is Ms. Jackson who is para 3.
She is having irregular contractions…"
She was not one of his regular patients.
Adem knew her as Sandy, who would bring
One of her many aunts, uncles, nephews,
Or nieces to the hospital for care.

He checked her and said, "You are not dilated.
You'll need hours to be ready to deliver.
You might as well send your husband to work."

1. I Am Pregnant but I Have no Husband

Sandy rolled her pretty eyes and focused
Them on Adem and defiantly said,
"I don't have a husband now and most likely
I won't have a husband in the future.
I can tell you why, but you won't understand.
You've been already brainwashed by half-truths,
And unfounded slanders of the white people.

"I ought to have a normal family.
My husband and I should work every day
To support our children, and school them right.
Surely, we should pay the hospital bills.
Well, I do not have what I ought to have.

2. I have Inherited no Riches

"Do not tell me that immigrants arrive
To this country without any money,
Still they prosper by hard work and thriftiness,
Without telling me that they come here rich
In family ties and family values.
Well, I have inherited no riches.

3. We Have to Change this Society

"Yes, Sir. I graduated from high school.
With that diploma I can be a maid
To rich white folks, and clean their daily filth.
When they are entertaining their white guests,
I can talk politely not to embarrass
My grandmaster and my fussy mistress.
With a smile I can say 'Yes Ma'am and Yes Sir.'
But I will not do that. I would rather sit
On my butt, and collect more welfare checks
And have more and more kids out of wedlock.
And I will let the white folks pay for their care,

Until the time I graduate from college,
And find a well-paying job for myself.
If they will not give a well-paying job
To this uppity black girl, then I will
Continue to collect what may be free.

"In fact what I may collect is not free,
It is back pay from whites to my ancestors.

"How do I know? That's all we talk about.
Remember, all we do is to collect welfare,
Get drunk, have sex and have more kids to draw
More child-support. So we have time to talk.
However, whites do not have time to listen.
Sooner or later they will have to listen.
Together, we must change this society.
Otherwise we must suffer together,
For we're weary of suffering alone.
The civil rights movement is gaining strength,
And growing fast even in the Deep South."

Adem said, "I am sorry Miss Jackson,
I did not mean to touch any sore spot
In a day that you'll have many sore spots."
"Doc, you are naïve, for what you desire
To happen won't happen to real people.
They say God loves us all, but *here and now,*
He loves some of His children more than others.
Hereafter, He might love them equally.

4. The Word of Love Has Many Meanings

"I have never been able to figure
Out what people mean when they talk of love.
Do they use it as a drug to tame us,
In order to get from us what they want?
Or is it a license for some people
To hurt us and then make restitution
By simply saying, 'I really love you'

"When a white girl is itching to be laid,
Would she say, 'I love you' to justify
Her intentions just before she drops her
Panties to make her pink lips accessible?

"Love is made of high peaks of happiness,
And deep canyons of long-drawn suffering.
Since suffering is not a significant
Part of the white culture, I wonder if whites
Could love as deep, or as high as black people.

"I am happy when my family is
Happy, and I suffer when they suffer.
This nurturing is love enough for me."

5. A New Life and a New Hope

When she was dilated, Adem called back.
He delivered a healthy boy who sucked
The cool ambient air into his lungs,
And announced his presence with a loud cry.
He was demanding attention and praise.

For Adem this infant could not be just
Another social security number.
In his mind, he gave a name to the child,
Bengal Tiger, and thought about his future.
He said to himself, "This boy will make it.
He possesses the strength and the stamina
To go the distance. The least he can do
Is to be a physician just like myself."

XXIX. How Far Can a Caged Bird Fly?
How Far Can a One Winged Bird Fly?

A few days after the birth of the boy,
Adem was returning about midnight
From a house party in St. Louis suburbs.
He was tailed and stopped by a policeman,
And charged with driving erratically;
Tested for alcohol intoxication.
He walked in a straight line and passed the test.

In the early fifties nobody thought
About intoxication due to drugs,
Though the seeds of drug problems were sprouting,
Which grew and multiplied in the sixties.

Adem told the policeman he was not
Acquainted with suburbs and his maps did
Not include them, as there were no landmarks,
He was forced to slow to read the street signs.
If he were to locate the Clayton Road,
He'd be able to find his way around.

The policeman gave him easy to follow
Directions and allowed him to proceed.
Since that was Adem's first encounter with
The law, he was tense. He drove in reverse,
And hit the patrol car with his rear bumper.
This time the official sounding policeman

Said, "You damaged the county's property.
You have to come to the police station."
He gave Adem directions as to which
Streets were the best to take to the station.
Adem said, "Sir, this all started because
I don't know the streets. Please, you lead the way,
And I will follow you to the station."
The policeman cautiously agreed and
Gave a warning, "Don't dare to run away!"

As he was following the police car,
The warning, "Don't dare to run away!" was
Resounding in his mind. Also, questions
Of his own: "How far can a caged bird fly?"
"How can a bee in a jar buzz or sting?"
Were echoing, and getting louder and louder.

At the station, he presented his driving
License and insurance papers and added,
"I could write a check for the damages."
They talked about a bail and some other
Legal jargons, and told him to wait for
Them to process an incident report.

While waiting he realized it was one
Of those times when the mind shows its
Outer shell while hiding its inner softness.

The hard facts hit him. He had nobody
To tell about his trivial problem.
He informed his insurance man by phoning.
But his helpful agent was less than friendly.
He felt alone without any supporter.

1. Tough Mind Looks for a Soft Place to Fall

His mind drifted back home, there the same scene
Was taking place, but he was not alone.
With self-assurance his father was barging

In as if he owned the police station,
Either by using his political
Clout or by paying for the damages,
His father was settling the incident.
On the way home he was saying, "The next
Time you run into a police vehicle,
Do not just dent it but demolish it.
So that I can see what my son can do."

The policeman set a court hearing date,
And let him go. As he drove to his quarters,
Once more his mind shifted back to his city.
He was in a courtroom between two lawyers
Who were his grandfather and his big brother.
They were pleading his case. He had no worries.

His grandfather learned the worth of words during
A half of a century of law practice.
Somehow if he could score a success with
A penny's worth of yes or no, he'd not
Spend a dollar's worth of legal jargon,
Which made him a whole without any seams.

2. Even the Stronger Needs Support

Then Adem's mind returned to the boy whom
He delivered a few days earlier.
Now he was not foreseeing his future
As bright as he had seen it earlier.
Though he can make it without the support
Of a father, but not without having
An empty space in his heart for a father.

All through his life, he has to swim with one
Arm stroke against the strong currents of life,
And has to fly with one wing against the winds.

When Adem reported to the courtroom,
One sentence was spoken, "The case is dismissed."

XXX.   The Color

Adem used to hear about the uniqueness
Of the blue color of the Aegean.
Back home they'd say, "There's no blue like its blue."
He'd say to himself, "The sea is the sea.
The blue is the color of any sea."
When he saw the Atlantic Ocean and
The Gulf of Mexico for the first time,
During a vacation at Galveston,
He could not judge what he saw with his eyes.
What kind of optical illusion made
The waters of these oceans so murky?
Why were the Gulf shores devoid of villas?

Even the skies were playing tricks on him.
The clouds were veiling the sun in a way
That he could not gauge its tanning power.
By the time he thought of getting a sunburn,
He already had second degree burns.
When he returned to his room just a patch
Of white skin was hiding under his trunks,
And the rest was red like the Turkish flag.
All night, he sipped liquids to hydrate himself,
To prevent an acute renal shut down.

After his return from Texas, the ocean
Sent its hurricanes to reclaim its shores.
Then he understood why the Americans
Were shunning the shores of the mighty oceans.

1. Haunting Images

Soon after returning to St. Louis what
He had seen became pleasing memories.
However, one image was haunting him.
The inscriptions on the public fountains
Boldly proclaiming; *For Whites; For Colored.*
Surely he had seen the signs on the walls
Of the public restaurants in St. Louis:
We reserve the right to refuse services
To any one. He had known what it meant,
But those signs were not singling out any
One race by name, and degrading their souls.

2. Charlie Nelson's Opinions on Slavery

One evening Adem visited Angilo's
To talk with Charlie Nelson where his mind
Would not be preoccupied with his work.
He led Charlie to a table, and brought
Up the subject of *For Whites…For Colored;*
And the feelings that whites still owe black people
Just back-pay for their enslaved ancestors.

Charlie, "Mankind went wrong a long time ago,
When he began to plunder and take slaves;
And to exploit his fellow human beings.
During the time of ancient Egyptians,
Greeks, Babylonians and Israelites
Slavery became an institution.

"By the time of the Trojan wars, taking
Slaves was not beastly even to the gods.
Greeks were beseeching without feeling guilt,
'Zeus most glorious and great, Thunder Cloud,
Throned in the heavens! Let not the sun go
Down and darkness come, until we cast down
Headlong the citadel of King Priam
In flames, and burn his gates with blazing fire.

Rip to rags the shirt upon Hector's breast.
May many of his men fall about him
Prone in the dry dust, and bite the brown earth.
Grant us absolute victory so that
We can take their yellow gold, white silver,
And gray iron. We can slaughter their men
And carry with us their wives and children,
By the big boat loads, into slavery.'

"Later on, a Greek philosopher, with
A great mind and a social consciousness,
Considered slavery as one of those
Necessary social evils of men.

"Slavery lasted several thousands
Of years due to absolute equality
Among the slaves, and their dynamic lives
In their slave quarters and communities.
They neither organized nor revolted.

"Only those slaves who were recently freed,
Or recently enslaved caused disorder.

"Men easily justified their evil
Deeds when they enslaved people belonging
To another race, tribe, nation or culture.
Yet, they did not mind much when they enslaved
Their neighbors and even their relatives.

"Christianity did nor bar slavery
For it preached servitude and dependence.
True Christians are made to be faithful slaves.
They know it and do not object it.
Thus they did not mind if blacks were enslaved."

3. America Already Made Reparation

"This Country inherited the defective
Gene of slavery from the old countries.

However, unlike any other country,
Throughout history, only this country
Made reparation by shedding the blood
Of her free men to abolish slavery.

"When a scorpion is surrounded by
A ring-of-fire, rather than burn to death,
It commits suicide by stinging itself.

4. Civil War

"A civil war is a ring-of-fire for
A state and its citizens feed on themselves.

"A soldier that you slay is your brother.
A maiden that you molest is your sister.
A house that you harry is your own home.
A city that you sack is your own city.
Riches that you rifle are your own riches.

"Slaves are free ever since our fathers fought,
Killed and got killed in a civil war.

5. Everyone Has to Make Decisions

"Even the slaves have to make decisions.
Aesop of Phrygia, Diogenes
Of Sinop, and Bilal of Mecca were
Slaves and all of them made decisions
As to how to conduct their affairs.

6. Equality

"What Blacks are asking is not the freedom,
Which they possess, but equality.
The South's '*Separate but Equal*' bias

Is a last-ditch effort; it is destined
To lose over time, and that time is now.

"The Civil Rights Movement is fit and thriving.
Since equality is the first condition
Of a free society, the law is
On the side of a full equality.
Although equality is not equal
To self-reliance and individual
Freedom—which comes through personal choices,
And personal responsibility.

7. I Refuse to Feel Guilt

"They say white people should be responsible
For their fathers having enslaved the blacks.
I don't feel any responsibility.
I refuse to feel guilt. It leads to hate.
As I have already said, our fathers
Paid their debt with their blood. And that is that.
As awful as it might be, slavery
Is an economic system in which
A slave master drives his slaves to work harder.
But he chooses to sustain and house them
As economically as possible.
The slaves work as little as they can,
And consume as much as it is possible.

"Once that ill-gotten system is abolished,
There's nothing left to save or to salvage.

"Then it is up to the freed slaves to find
A promised-land, and build a beautiful
City and a high tower for themselves."

XXXI. The Same Old Problems and New Reactions

When Adem finished his internship, Ann
Said, "This calls for a celebration.
I'll pick you up this evening." She arrived
With a new car, and drove to a new place.
They passed quickly through the crowd, and they chose
A corner table where the lights were dim,
And the sound of the music was soothing.

That night her voice was not just melodious,
But her words were chosen to make a point.

"I should be happy with my brand new car,
Well I'm not. I was shopping for a Chevy.
I found the right color and the options
I preferred, but the car dealer would not
Sell the car with my signature alone.
He asked that my husband be a cosigner.
So I bought a Ford instead of a Chevy.
I have a longer work record than his.
He just finished the law school with GI
Bill benefits and with my resources.
He has a long way to go before he
Can establish a lucrative law practice.

"This country is dominated by men.
Look, at the top of any corporation
Or government-post all you see are men.

"According to fictitious etiquette.
A husband should treat his wife like a queen,
In fact, she's a keeper of man's possessions—
She's being the top prize who's unemployed.

"Women workers are valuable to fill
The vacuum created by male absence.
During the war women had gainful jobs,
Then they slipped back into the hands of men.
The war is over and once more the women
Are being asked to stand behind their men.
It would be a queenly life-work if their
Men were to keep standing in front of them.

"When a father makes a profound statement:
'I'd like to keep family name going.'
Watch out girls! He is plainly pronouncing,
'I'd like to give to my sons the largest
Portion of the family fortune.'

"I am worried about my marriage too.
When his political ambitions will
Possess him, I am not at all certain
That I'll be suited to stand behind him.
I won't be the first pretty face who is
Left far behind. But I won't be caught napping.

"When he builds his practice, I will not ask
Him to buy a house for me in the suburbs.
Suburbs are changing this society,
Where women are isolated and bored.
Instead, I will get him to pay for my
MA and for my Ph.D. degrees.
Today he is out of town, being primed
For a future political career.

"What's more this country has a double standard,
And the man has all the advantages.
If someone would notice my husband
With a pretty woman in a hotel,

All he's doing is making new connections
That might boost his career in the future.
When a woman is seen under the same
Circumstances, she's having an affair.

"Knowing about a certain fact and choosing
Not to talk about it won't change that fact.
When Kinsey wrote about the sexual
Behavior of men, clergy and the keepers
Of the traditions were infuriated—
Not with the facts, but that somebody was
Daring to write about such a subject.

"Women are churning deep down and learning
To cherish their daughters just like their sons.
They are now sowing the seeds, and their daughter
Will harvest the fruits of their labor.

"In this country, only teaching, nursing,
And secretarial professions are
Held by women and they come with low wages.

"Yet we women are metamorphosing.
As men had seen the light for the first time
When they came out of the womb of women,
They will see the light for the second time
When they dare to come out of their cocoons.

"This society wants women to bear
And rear children, yet they are penalized
For doing what only women can do.

"You know Nurse Ruth Jones, from Poplar Bluff,
When she just conceived, she got a small loan,
And paid it back long before it was due.
When she needed to get another loan
During the last months of her pregnancy;
The loan was denied for she was showing.

"Mrs. Mansfield, the Head Nurse, is a sweet
And stately lady. She's an exquisite
Example of a nurse of bygone days.
She keeps her uniforms starched and snow-white.
She obeys the orders of attending
Physicians as if their words were the law.
She treats male interns with love and affection.
When they are on duty, during the night,
She won't wake them up for petty problems.
When she must call, then pampers them with treats,
For they're her surrogate sons who made good.
When they make a mistake, she gently guides them.

"But she is brash with female physicians.
She thinks they are getting to big for their
Breeches and losing their femininity.
She bosses the nurses whom she manages.

"She practices differently than us.
During her first evening rounds, she assesses
And restrains those patient who might fall.
She then feeds them and then medicates them.
Her last round is to pass the sleeping pills.
While her patients are seeing sweet dreams,
Her shift is over without any incident."

Their conversation channeled into its
Own channel running smoothly and swiftly.

What was important for them was the flow
Of conversation with its dancing ripples,
And the natural music of those ripples.

They knew what was hidden beneath the surface;
However, they were reluctant to stir
The calm waters and let the feelings surface.

XXXII.   The Advice of the Heart

While Adem was keeping his feelings under
Control with his intellect, his heart was
Going out of control, it was running
Faster and faster, pausing for a moment
Not to rest but to gain more speed to jump
Over the fence, and to land on Ann's side.

The heart continued to skip a few beats
Just to put a few words in Adem's ears,
"The brain put you on a treadmill to run
Without allowing you reach any place;
I must be terse for I can't take my time
To spin a tall tale as the brain can.
The brain's long snaky words are hard to grasp.
After their heads are crushed, their tails keep wiggling.

"I want you to use only monosyllabic
Words with a single well-defined meaning.
They are like bullets. Either they will hit
The target and the outcome is obvious,
Or they'll miss the target, and the result
Is a vexing vibration in your ears.

"As gunpowder must be dry and granular,
Let your words have room to breathe lest they clump.

"Let your target be a tangible one,
The types that you can smell, taste, touch, and feel.
That way you'll know whether you hit or miss.

"Once you voice your words, let them do their deeds.
I do not want you to define, defend,
Retrieve, or reclaim any one of them.
Let them stand naked without modifiers,
For all to see their beauty or ugliness.

"Do you hear me? This is your heart that's speaking.
I do not want you to give names to your words.
Let them find their own names and be neutral
Whether they are labeled, lies, lust, or love.

"Think of her not as a prey who's running,
But as a huntress who's plotting to pounce.
Who are you? The hunter, or the quarry?
As I see it, in the play of lovers
There is no hunter or hunted for both
Lovers play the both roles over and over.

"Be careful, she has many concealed weapons;
She may give you hope with a smile without
Giving anything substantial at all,
Or chose to paralyze you with a frown.
She may sigh such a way to drain your sap,
She may shed pearls to neutralize your power.
She may snare you with a strand of her hair
And drag you to any place she may choose.
When she is bored, she may give the deathblow
By piercing your heart with a single eyelash.

"Come out of your comfortable cocoon.
You ought to have naught to hide from your lover.
If you are afraid of festering wounds
It's the time to wind your springs to spring back.

"Come out of your shell. Spill your inner passions.
Say, the time is now and the place is this place.
Say, I am born right now. I have no past.
Say, I do not count on my days to come.
Say, I came from no place. I go no place.
Say, This is a free space where I stand fast.

Say, I am rich, for I have nil to lose.
Say, I do not fear that I may be scorned.
Say, my choice of words may be the wrong ones,
For there's no one who can chose the right words.
Sweet words may grow sour and sour words may ripen.

"See the spark of life in her eyes and then
Say, your spark has the hues of blues and greens.
Say, I want to be torched with your spark now.
Then bring up the smooth skin, flesh, blood, and bones.
Speak of her red lips, pink cheeks, lush blond hair,
Swan neck, firm breast, thin waist line, and long legs.
Hold your head near her to hear her heartbeats,
And to feel her fresh breath on your bare neck,
Turn your nose near her skin to smell her scent.
Tune your ears to her voice. Heed to her grace.
Don't think. Let the voice of your heart guide you."

Those tiny words stuck to his vocal cords.
If those small words were to choke him to death
He could not cough them up to save his life.

He looked into the mirror of her eyes,
And saw the likeness of the words of heart.
To break the silence he said, "Ann, why does
A man dreams of what lies beyond the bliss?"

When they began to dance, with every step,
Supple steel was twining with silky softness.
They were generating and gathering
Energy by wrapping and unwrapping
Around each other and absorbing each
Other's force to heighten their potency.

When the vibration of music grew still,
They drove into the darkness of the night.
The veil of darkness veiled their flaming fire.

Ann and Adem's oneness, without any
Space between them, did not start and thrive

Like a love affair of two young lovers.
Their bond was born without being conceived,
Without going through a gestation time,
And without suffering any birth pangs.
It reached its maturity without having
Growing pains of adolescence period.

They were one like two bulbs of an hourglass.
As the sands of their whole being ran from
One bulb into the other one, they neither
Gained nor lost a single grain of their being.
They were destined to be one, and each one
Destined to keep his/her identity.

Since their oneness was formless and shapeless,
Each passing year could not warp, or chip its
Edges to turn them jagged to hurt them.
It was born nameless and remained nameless.
Let the others guess whether they had many
Past lives together to perfect their bonds
Into pure love or let them call it lust.

Romantic love with its adrenaline
Rush is a physiological function.
And with its romance it is an illusion.

Love acts as the mortar to fill the gap
Between two lovers to bind them together.
When love loses its adhesive power,
Then the lovers roll down like two stones coming
Down from a peek to find their resting places.
Once more the love between souls takes over,
That is, if it were there in the first place.

XXXIII. The Analysis of Internship

Adem thought of his internship and said,
"I've learned everything I needed to learn.
What I might learn from now on is a sequel.

"Life is the greatest creation of God
Who will lend it to us for a short while
To do our deeds, then He will take it back.
This gift of life is both a beginning
And a certain end for any mortal.

"If we don't revere life and hold it sacred
What else could be valued in the cosmos?

"The physician is not an artist for
He can't pick and choose his medium that's
Suited to create his masterpiece;
Still he's privileged to go near the sacred
Canvas of life to do minor touch-ups.
He is not a judge for he can't judge
As to who's worthy to live and who's not.

"There is no allowance for human slip,
For each individual patient is
Either one hundred per cent live or not.

"The birth and death are natural happenings,
But suffering and misery are not.
When one can't cure, one must soothe the suffering.

"To be ready to respond at any
Hour of the day is a part of the package,
For sickness won't wait to strike at set hours.

"Personal lives of the people are like
A chain which is made of old and new links
Of success and failure, gladness and sorrow,
Bliss and blight, and love and disillusionment.

"Old links may be covered with dust and rust
Nonetheless, they are a part of the chain.
Linking a new link is just one more link.
It cannot take the place of the old one.
The link of Nuran's love was in its place;
Lately written poems in English could
Not dislodge the ones written in Turkish.

"One must realize that life is too precious
To waste it by trying to be a winner.
One has to learn not to push one's way through,
But to take the way and follow it through."

During the next five years of his training
He sailed leisurely on the placid seas.
Ardor of hard work hardly rocked his boat.

XXXIV. Basic Science Researchers

Adem's research was designed to glean data
On cancer at the molecular level.
His colleagues were basic science researchers.
He thought these people were a mutant breed:
Suspicious, secretive, selfish, curious,
Although, surprisingly intelligent.

As a child, they either had never learned
To share or they had shed their faculty
Of sharing before entering a lab.
Yet they've dreamt the same dream: *The Nobel Prize*.

They've relied on hard work and clung to luck.
When something went wrong with their experiment,
They simply sacrificed a few more rats.
There were no lawyers around chasing lab
Carts to sue them on behalf of their victims.

For them cancer was a man-eating monster
That had to be slain as a trophy.
Although for the basic science researchers
Suffering did not have a human face.
They've stood for the numbers to be compiled
For their statistical analyses,
Which proved that the cancer was killing less
People than it was feeding researchers.

XXXV.   Mutual Understanding Grows into Love

One researcher, Gale Gibson, kept her mother's
Picture on her workbench, and she attempted
To track down her mother's killer: *The Cancer.*

The two researchers, Gale and Adem were
Working on two distinct fractions of histones.
To purify their proteins, they had
To use similar techniques, and they were
Willing to share their skills with each other.

Gale, a Ph.D. biochemist, had
A keen knowledge of amino acids.
When she'd talk about the single or double
Peptide bonds, one would feel that she was bringing
Those theoretical bonds into life.

In time…they saw a new facet of love
In each other, which led them into marriage.
A son, Orhan, and a daughter, Ayhan,
Added two extra bonds of their union.

XXXVI. The Chemistry of the People

The family returned to Istanbul.
Gale discovered that basic chemistry
Of people was the same around the world.

A warm smile would trigger a reaction,
And a little added kindness would quicken
That reaction to generate goodwill.

She was in need of a special friendship.
When she developed that friendship between
Her husband and herself, attaching it
To her love and marriage, she developed
A final product that would not melt under
The heat, or crack under the freeze of life.

When the kids were young, they moved back and forth
With ease between the old and new country.
When children required a firm ground to grow,
They settled down in the Western U.S.

XXXVII.   Still a Wayfarer

Adem kept busy with medical practice,
Although he allotted time to himself
For classical and modern poetry.
Later on, he realized that reading
Old epic poetry was reflecting
Only a distorted shadow of man,
Which was cast upon the canvas of nature.

His patients' unedited books of life
Were available for him to pore over.
Though prologues and epilogues of those books
Were the same, the middle chapters were filled
With shades of their personal love and loss,
Or pain and pleasure which made them unique.

The study of philosophy and science,
Methodically guided him to the border
Of the unknown, and left him standing there.
He had to penetrate into the realm
Of the unknown to find light in its mazes.

He studied the main paths of many faiths,
And every one of them faithfully guided
Him to the door of God, and left him there.

He found the tip of the tangled up thread
Of Truth and untangled it to free himself
From the web of man-made rules and rituals.

He came out of his conventional self,
And lost the sense of political borders,

And human conception of ownership.
He freed himself from two enslaving
Shackles of the human spirit and mind:
The illusion of imminent mishap,
And the false hope of forthcoming good fortune.

XXXVIII.   The Path of the Soul

In search of a direct path to the Source
He listened to the universal message,
Which is being broadcast all through the ages.

He let the inward-pulling cosmos pull
Him inwards to grasp the things inwardly
To merge with the cosmos all around him.

He whispered into the vast universe,
And it echoed back to him through the love
Songs of birds and the chirping of crickets.
He saw the invisible thread that goes
Through every atom in the universe,
He was able to grasp that eternal
Thread, thereby, he linked himself with all things.

He would drive through the undulating fields
Of the Palouse country where the land is
So youthful that it has neither lost its
Fertility nor its curvaciousness.
The wheat would bow their heads and he'd bow back.
He would wander through the apple orchards
Of Wenatchee and millions of red or
Gold cheeks would smile at him, and he'd smile back.
He'd tease them, "How do you extract your red
And gold from the brown earth and colorless water?"

Simple and straightforward questions no longer
Had a preconceived straight and simple answers.

When he would stop at a roadside fruit stand,
An angel-faced teenage girl would hear his
Accent and she'd ask, "Where are you from, Mister?"
It'd break his trance, but he'd still feel as though
He were jolted and he'd have no quick answer.
Saying, '*I'm from Turkiye,*' would sound shallow.
Telling the truth, '*I'm a part of the cosmos.*
I carry the essence of distant stars
In my body, and wherever I happen
To stand it's my country,' would sound too deep.
To satisfy the curiosity
Of an innocent youth, he devised his
Travelers lie, "I'm from the old country."

He bought a box of apples and began
To probe them from stem-end to blossom-end.
Their plump cheeks were reddish at the center,
But at the periphery the color
Faded to pinkish gold, and then to whitish.
Their specks of russets made them look exotic;
They resembled freckled-faced playful girls.

He was pleased with the quality of apples,
But did not ask as to which tree bore them.

XXXIX. The Water, the Bull Elk and the Round Rock

Adem developed a special affection
For Lake Pend Oreille for it goes deeper,
For the Clark Fork River for it is swifter.
He'd meet with the Clark Fork at the Cabinet
Gorge where the river would grow receptive.

Years ago while hiking in the Cabinet
Gorge, he noticed the hoof prints of an elk
On the scanty earth covering the rocks.
He tracked down the hoof prints, which led the way
To a high and dry ledge, and the ledge came
To a dead-end on an immense round rock.
Below the rock there was the churning white waters
That was too sunken for the elk to reach.
Above the rock there was a lofty cliff,
Which was impossible for it to climb.
Adem thought that the elk must have been lost,
For there was nothing there for him to drink,
Nor was there any forage to range over.
Yet, each time he would visit the vista,
He would come upon the same fresh hoof prints.
Later on, Adem met with that Bull Elk.
Then he realized that the Bull Elk was
Purposely frequenting the same vista
Point for the same reason as he himself:
Not to drink, not to graze but just to be
There to watch the scenery and to prove
The point that he was a part of the whole.
They chose the Round Rock as their meeting place.

In time the Round Rock grew closer toward
Them and began to talk, "I react slowly,
For I am energy that's crystallized.
And yet there's action where there's energy.
Constantly energy grows into matter,
And the matter turns into energy.
In this self-contained cosmos naught is lost.
This backward and forward flow is the whole.
This is the known mystery of the cosmos.

"I am not aloof toward you fellows:
Regardless of our outer shells, cosmic
Forces change us while the eternity
Stands still in one place without ever changing.
It is an illusion that makes us think
That the eternity is changing while
We are the ones who are constantly changing.
What we call good or evil is nothing
More or less than the display of forces.
Birth and death are but merely two links on
The long chain of constant change of forces.

"In this universe wanderers won't cover
Any more grounds than the ones who stand still.
I remain where I was born yet I'm as
Equally blessed or cursed as the wanderers.

"The rain bathes me and the summer sun's direct
Rays come down to towel and to dry me.
The snow blankets me, but the winter sun's
Tangential rays punch holes in my blanket
To let the water soak into my pores.
Then comes the northerly with its fury,
Whistling through the gully to turn the soft
Water in my pores into expending
Wedges to tear my skin and cells apart.
Then comes the warm rains of spring to wash my
Eroded scales and cells down the river.

"The thick moss that clothes my naked body,
And the delicate wild flowers that honor
My crown are nothing less than pestilence.
They cling on me, just to suck my substance.
They also, cause the change that gives me life.

"The cosmic forces are at work to cause change.
We think of these changes as curse or blessings
According to the seasons of our lives.

"Please visit with me as frequently as you can.
I'm getting smaller by each passing day.
A few billions years hence, I won't be here."

Adem and the Bull Elk kept wandering,
Yet they missed what was nearer to them.
By standing still and expending their souls
They have reached to the end of the cosmos.

The Bull Elk and Adem chose the Round Rock
As the exact center of their universe.
They merged with each other and with the cosmos.
Consequently, they felt at home at any
Place they happen to be at that moment.

Making friends and keeping them was easy.
They rated animosity no more
Than a passing wintry wind between friends.

As the years passed by, the events took place,
Though Adem did not call them good or evil.
No longer did terrible things frighten him,
Nor did good fortune cast a spell on him.

XL. Looking Backwards to Live Forwards

Adem looked back to see how far he's journeyed.
Since he broke up with his fiancée Nuran,
That phase of his life was at a standstill.
He has never made an attempt to see
Her face, nor to hear her voice as much as
On the phone, nor to see a recent picture
Of her, nor to see her recent handwriting.

He kept her in his mind forever young.
She stayed wrinkle free, her voice never cracked,
Her mind stayed sharp, and her poise never wavered.

Adem and Nuran kept in touch through their
Mutual friends and through their publications.
Friends said that Nuran was not the same ever
Since she lost her sixteen-year-old daughter
In the black bowels of the Bosphorus
While she was defending her title as
"The Cross Boshporus Swimming Champion."
They said that Nuran takes care of her patients,
And runs her research lab, but she can't keep schedules.
She smiles as before, but the jagged edges
Of grief pierce through the veil of her smiles.
She blames herself for her daughter being
So talented, and for nurturing her
So that her daughter's talents could drown her.

She'd says, "How could I have been so blind not
To see the nature of the Bosphorus,
While it'd been known by men since ancient times.

"Its bare beauty is accentuated
By its shores in Europe and Asia.
When a man looks from one side of its shores,
He thinks that the other half of the heaven
Is lying at the far side of its shores.

"Long before memory, men have been crossing
The Bosphorus with a deep-seated desire
To possess the other half of the heaven.

"The Bosphorus is the token dividing
Line between Europe and Asia, which
Fostered hatred between shores' people,
And they've crossed the line to hurt each other.

"In time, men changed but not the Bosphorus.
It's not a little finger of the sea,
In fact it's made of two mighty currents:
One riding over the other and each
One is running in an opposite course;
Brackish and lighter waters of the Black
Sea layer at the surface and runs south,
While the salty, heavy and warm waters
Of the Marmara runs north at the bottom.

"Each current makes way for the other one,
But now and then one of them collides with
The sinuous cost line eddies and swirls,
And upsets the balance between the two.
Then both streams cause devilish countercurrents
To veer from clockwise to counterclockwise
To tear and pull everything down to drown.
Then once again the balance is restored.

"Today's precarious balance was reached
At the end of the last glacial epoch.
The Black Sea was a calm fresh water lake.
Its level was several hundred feet
Below that of the Mediterranean.
Then one day the Mediterranean
Popped the cork at the Bosphorus and emptied
Its salty waters into the Black Sea,
Creating a water fall two hundred
Times the volume of Niagara Falls.

Since she had a turbulent past, she learned
To flaunt her fair face while hiding her fury.

"Once Jason and his Argonauts had sailed
Through it in their quest for the Golden Fleece.
Darius I had first bridged it with pontoons.
Fatih blocked it to choke the Byzantine.

The Ottomans renamed the Bosphorus
As Istanbul Bogazi—Throat of Istanbul—
For it had given breath to the empire.

"All those great men, Fatih, Darius I,
And Jason had help to achieve their goals,
But my daughter attempted to succeed,
Using her ability and powers."

Ann and Adem were never separated
Because they were like two trees, which happened
To take roots and to grow next to each other.
With each fall of their lives, they'd lose their leaves
And could not kiss each other leaf to leaf,
But their tangled roots were always in touch.

Ann's prediction of carnage came to pass.
She lost a husband in the Vietnam War
And a brother returned barely alive.

XLI. Echoes of the Past on the Great Wall of China

Adem visited China to see how
Far men would go to build shells around them.
As he was wandering on the Great Wall,
He heard the echoes of his inner voice,
"I was the stern king Shih Huang-ti.
I built most of these lofty wall to shield
Myself with an impenetrable shell.
I was the mason and the hod carrier.
I was also the peasant and I worked
My terraced rice paddies to raise just
Enough rice to feed the starving laborers.
I paid my meager taxes so the king
Could pay miserly wages to the workers.

"I was the Turk ruling north of the wall.
At that time, I called myself Hsiung-Nu.
The wall was built to keep me out of China.
But I found many gaps in the thick wall
And penetrated deep into China.

"Conquering China was easy but keeping
The Chinese under control was difficult.
The Chinese had a way of slowly gnawing
Away and digesting any conqueror.

"The Chinese soldiers' swords could not slash me.
However, the soft skins of Chinese girls
And soft silk of their looms softened me.
I completely lost my identity
When I called my children by Chinese names.

"To reclaim myself I went to the north.
I strengthened my body in Baykal Lake,
Heightened my spirits at the Altay Mountains
And regained my unconquerable courage.

Before long the western world enticed me.
I conquered most of Europe and Turkiye.

"Then I returned to the north of the Wall.
The previous gaps in the Wall were sealed,
But this time I found even wider gaps,
And once again I invaded China."

A whispering voice came through the thin lips
Of a Chinese Guide, "Where are you from, Mister?"
I heard myself saying, "From the New World."

XLII.   Back to the Cabinet Gorge

Adem was eagerly getting ready
To embark on the last leg of his journey.
He had been living in Spokane longer
Than any other place on this planet.
It was the right time for him to move on.

Once more, Adem visited the Round Rock.
It was living its life where it was born,
And gaining more wisdom without wandering.
He too sat still to see the world around.

An eagle was occupying his throne,
And keeping his eyes on his vast domain.
Although in his mind's eye Adem's was seeing
The European white stork who can't soar
Like an eagle to catch her prey in flight,
Can't pluck a fish from a lake as she flies,
Can't screech to send shivers into the hearts
Of small lives on the ground or in the sky.

Since the stork is mute, she could not wail when
Jesus was crucified but she shed tears.

In the fall, ahead of the cold winters
In Europe, while she returns to Africa,
She makes her fall pilgrimage to Jerusalem.
In the spring, while she returns to Europe,
She makes her yearly pilgrimage to Mecca,
Before she takes her proper place upon
The chimneys to be close to the children.

Nevertheless, she calls herself neither
An African nor a European.

Thinking about the mute stork brought back his
Muted and half-forgotten childhood memories.
When one is a little child, his storehouse
Of memories are completely empty.
When the adults reminisce by saying,
"Ten years ago…" He tries to retrieve some
Sort of memories; yet he recalls nothing.

The present is like the neck of an hourglass,
Through which sands of time pass too fast for him
To observe actually what is happening.
But the future is palpable and real.
The kind of person that he hopes to grow
Into and the things that he hopes to have
Are in the future for him to attain.

When Adem was twelve, during an earthquake,
He was jolted by electricity,
Which gave him a near death experience.
His past passed by in a split second.
Whereas the future that he knew little
Of extended into eternity.

He measured the facts by the thimbleful
As they had happened. Either he did not
See the options or could not measure them.

When the Siberian winds whistled during
The harsh winters, he endured it,
Not knowing that summery days were being
Enjoyed just south of the Taurus Mountains.
When the rays of the summer sun would hit
The cobblestones of the streets, they would leave
The heat behind by moving to their summer
Home at the foothills of Mt. Erciyes.
He knew no other place that was cooler.

An infant tightly grasps an object that
Is put into his hands and won't let go.
A child quickly feels a new object with
One hand while he maintains his tight grip with
The other hand on a thing that is known.

To youth facts are distinct with clear edges:
Virtuous people won't have any vice,
People with vice won't have any virtue.
As they open and closes the doors of facts,
They discover that those doors swing both ways.

XLIII.   The Pilgrimage Back Home

Adem realized that he was journeying,
On a level path. The scenery was
Beautiful but there was nothing thrilling.
He wished to have a resting-place to get
Ready for the next leg of his journey.
He asked permission of the earth. She said,
"I have refused no one. You too are welcome."

He made a pilgrimage to his birthplace
To see it once more with his worldly eyes.
In the city of Kayseri he found
Nothing that was homey or familiar.
Even under the hot midsummer sun,
Mt. Erciyes was wearing her white scarf.

Old inns were torn down in order to make
Room for modern but faceless high-rise hotels.
Friendly innkeepers were replaced with
English speaking and schooled hotel managers
Who were experts on managing a hotel,
And they would not waste their breath with chitchat
As the old innkeeper, Osman Efendi
Would have done by habit, "You remember
Old Kurtoglu, may his soul rest in peace.
His two sons are now running his business.
Recently they were my guests in my inn.
I told them, 'Your dad and I go way back.
The same rules will apply to you as well.
In case you run short of cash let me know.

I may not have it but I have good friends
In the money and all of them owe me."

He hired a cab for the length of his stay.
The cabdriver was a most likely lad,
With a typical Kayserian accent, he said
That his name was Yasar Yesiloglu.
Adem asked him to drive to the old town.

When they arrived at Adem's neighborhood
He was not able to recognize it.
He searched for the single-family homes
With black basalt foundations, gray tuff walls,
And spacious courtyards but found none of them.

The volcanic ashes of Mt. Erciyes,
Under the weight of time, turned into tuff,
Which could be easily cut and polished,
And be turned into the bones of the city.
The tuff used to serve as a natural
Bridge between Mt. Erciyes and people.

Now the steel and concrete buildings were standing
As squatters on the sites of old houses.
And the people who live in them had no
Connections with the nature around them.

Adem said to Yasar, "Please drive away,
Take me around the city as you please,
For I have no other destination."

Adem continued to search for spinach
Fields and apricot orchards but found none.
The salt flats as well as marshlands were covered
With high-rise apartments and black top streets.

Creek beds were dry, no freely running springs,
They were imprisoned in pipes, and aquifers
Were pumped dry to meet the needs of the houses.

The outer city walls had disappeared.
Their foundations were swallowed by the soil.
Only a few sections were protruding
Above the ground like dinosaur fossils.
The inner walls and castle were restored,
Not just to keep invaders at bay
And to house and feed the people inside,
But to trap the tourists inside the walls
In order to cheat them in the new stores.

For several days, he stayed in the hotel
To probe his feelings and accept the fact
That what he had seen was not the same city.

XLIV.   What Is and Is not a City?

The city is not just its living people
Who may come and go, but it is also
The legends and myths that are left behind.

The city is not its outer or inner
Walls, public buildings, temples or its dwellings.
They can be built, then ruined or burned down,
Yet blackened stones, charred wood and ashes left
Behind can connect the past with the future.

Kayseri has no fixed city limits.
Mt. Erciyes is the city itself.
Her deep snow and her thin glaciers feed
Her springs and replenish her aquifers.
Her highlands with her flocks supply the wool
For the looms of the city where it flowers
Into the broad canvases of rugs.

The natural music of the city
Is the echoes of the calls of the male
Partridge, which is an invitation for the hen
And a warning for another male partridge.

The majesty of the city is the eagle
That keeps an eye on the hills and highlands.

The sweet scent of the city is the thyme.
The city is the scent of apricot
Blossom, which is the certain sign of spring.

The roots of the city are the deep roots
Of wild pears, scrub oak trees, and chokeberries
Which grow so deep that they can't be uprooted.

The city is the fertile foot hills that
Provide ground, for the vineyards and orchards.

The city is the brackish lakes with their
Migrant mallards, geese and resident carp.

The city is the marshlands with its rush,
Reed, weed, water buffalo, and white stork.

The city is the stony plains that grow
Vegetables and grains; wheat to feed the rich,
Rye to feed the poor, and barley to feed
The beast of burden, and other livestock.

The city is the people who know how
To blend, with basic life-supporting things.

XLV.   Yasar's Understanding of Man

As Yasar drove, he talked and Adem listened.
"After I finished high school, I started
To work as an apprentice truck driver,
For an international company
That hauled merchandise to and from Baghdad
And Tehran to European Countries.
The industrial centers of the West
Germany were the choice destinations.

"My master would not allow me to put
My hands on any driving wheel until
I had mastered the most complex machine.
According to him that machine was man.
He said, 'Men are honest but they would like
To receive a little bit more than they had
Bargained for, and they would like to deliver,
A bit less than they had pledged to provide.

'When you are balancing your business books
Never be generous with your partners,
Don't be ashamed to fight over a penny,
And be lavish after you close the books.'

"I turned the truck's cab into a library.
I began with a stack of foreign-language
Tapes and kept adding new ones, and kept learning.
When I became an independent driver,
I knew where and when to stop, and which country
To avoid if I had an alternative.

"Although I was already a seasoned driver,
During one of my long distance haul, I could
Not avoid going through Northern Italy.
What's more, I made a stop to check the tires.

"The only thing I could recall was seeing
A shadow standing behind me—that's all.
When I happened to regain consciousness,
I had a lump at the back of my head,
Dim vision, and a nauseating headache.

"I had only my work cloths on my back:
But my pockets were empty and no truck.
Somehow I found myself at Verona.
I informed the cops about the hijacking,
Simply I never heard a word from them.

"I needed support to recuperate
From my physical and mental trauma.
A Jewish man gave the help that I needed.
He took me in and nursed me back to health.
When I recovered, he made the arrangements,
For me to return to Turkiye.

"I expressed my gratitude for his act
Of kindness, and asked how much I owed him.
He said, 'My ancestors were saved by the Turks
From the Spanish Inquisition by giving
Them a haven in the Ottoman Empire.

'They lived in Izmir for generations.
My father's business required to move to
A new location, he moved to Italy.
His love of Izmir was always alive.

'For you being hijacked, injured, and left
In a foreign country without any
Support system was a hell to go through;
For me it was an opportunity
To make a payment on family's debt.'

"I learned then that there are two kinds of men:
The decent men and the indecent men.
I've found both kinds right here in Kayseri,
And ever since I've had no need to wander."

XLVI.   Pilgrimage to Akgelin's Sanctuary

Adem was about to leave Turkiye,
But not before making one last pilgrimage.
He asked Yasar to come at next dawn
With a Jeep to drive him to Mt. Erciyes.
By the time they'd reached Tekir Pass the sun
Was shimmering upon the Tekir Spring.
It is the highest spring of the highlands.
It was running as clear and as cool as ever.
Adem said, "Yasar, go to Kayseri,
And come back every few days at high noon.
If I am not sitting by the spring side
Do nothing—First of all don't search for me."

Pass the ski runs, he slowed and checked his bearings,
Convinced that he was on the right steep trail
To reach the Sacred Grounds of Akgelin.
He was stepping on those spent basalts ever
Carefully knowing that one nonchalant
Step could cause an avalanche of loose rocks
That would bury everything under them.

He reached his destination at sunset.
Geographically, the sanctuary
Was a collapsed dome and a spent caldera.
It was surrounded by lofty cliffs.

Just to the north of the caldera cliff
There was a precipice that could inflict
Height sickness even on seasoned climbers.

Next to the south cliff there was an ancient
Temple that was swallowed by thick layers
Of earth and fallen rocks save for its dome,
This could be seen when the snow has melted.
The temple was built at that elevation
By the Hittites in order to locate
Their sacred tablets closer to the gods.

The west cliff was less steep; it had a gap
That functioned as a gate to the caldera.

The east cliff was the steepest, which gave
Passage into a deep cave with a pool.
Akgelin's statue stood at the entrance.

The caldera had a microclimate
Of its own during the winter or summer.
It escapes the effect of severe weather.

Telling the facts about Akgelin's grounds,
Tell little about the myth of Akgelin.

It's said that once upon a time a young
Mother was escaping, clutching her arms
Around her two babies, and desperately
Searching for a secluded hiding place.
The chasing soldiers were right at her heels.
When she entered into the caldera,
She was trapped; having no way to escape,
And not willing to surrender, she willed
Herself and her babies to turn into stone.

It is said that she is an immortal.
The statue that stands in front of the cave
Is the outer shell of her family.
When the soldiers left the place, she walked trough
The stones and is still alive today.

She's just like Hizir, the immortal man,
Who helps any living being in need.
Above all she has an extra compassion
For women and children in need of help.
Some say she is the reincarnation
Of *Kubaba*—The Hittite Mother Goddess—

No one really knows her identity,
Or her nationality. Whom had she
Displeased? Why were the soldiers chasing her?

Everyone agrees the Grounds of Akgelin
Is a sanctuary for living things.
There can be no conflict in there but peace.

Old trees live there without fearing the ax,
For lumberjacks leave their axes outside
Before stepping in the sanctuary.

The wolf chases the deer, upon entering
The sanctuary, they become related.
The dove and eagle perch next to each other
On Akgelin's statue and they are friends.

Adem went into the cave and sat down.
He might not have believed in all those tales
About Akgelin that he has heard since
His childhood, yet during his youth when he
Had a problem he used to pay a visit
To the sanctuary and feel much better.
His problems would have their own solutions.

Adem was inspired with the peacefulness
And the mystical aura of the grounds.
He attained a youthful zest for life.

XLVII. The Meditation of Adem in the Cave

To get ready for his meditation,
He took a ritual bath in the pool.
He built a circle of rocks around himself.
He said a silent prayer of thanksgiving,
Not a supplication, to purify
His breath and blew over the rocks to keep
Enshrouded negative powers at bay.

"Dear God, You have a whole cosmos to run
Yet Your power cannot be exhausted
By performing miraculous achievements.
You still have the ability to see
When a black ant moves during a dark night
And hear the creaking of its ankle joint.

"I trust wonderful things are happening
In Your life-supporting other planets,
But I will not ask about them before
I can understand what's going on here.

"I have to confess that I am a sinner.
Regretfully, without any good reason,
I hurt some of your children—snakes and spiders.

"According to clerics I am a sinner.
They say I do not pray as it's prescribed.
I can't be sure if they are right or wrong,
For I am saying the same prayers that
They'd me memorize when I was a child.
I must confess, I did not know the meaning

Of my prayers then; I still don't know now.
But with your wisdom, I am sure you do.

"Forgive me Lord, sometime I question Your way
Of doing things and I find it unfair.
I say, He gave two legs and wings to some,
Four legs, claws, set of teeth and tail to some,
Two legs, two arms and a big brain to some,
No arms, no legs and no wings to the snake.

"Then I travel sixty millions years back,
I see no big-brained ones running around
But I see the snake gliding by feeling
The Mother Earth with its entire body
And thriving by being in tune with nature.

"Dear God, I have no problem with Your creatures
For they are admirable as they are
And they fit into the great scheme of things.
If You were to grant me the potency
To change their lots in a natural setting,
Without the man's meddling, I'd change nothing.

"Except that I have a problem with man.
He thinks, he is above the natural laws.
Consequently, this arrogance and pride
Of man will be the cause of his ruin.

"If the man were to race with the legless
Snake toward a finish line that is set
In the future, I'd bet on snake to win.

"For a long time, man has been dominated
By the needs of his Self, not of his Soul.
Through his selfishness, he has been acting
Not as one of Your children among others,
But as a master of his brothers.

"As you can see, man left no room to roam,
On this planet, for the rest of Your children.

He knows, snake takes one meal and it's satisfied
For several weeks. It will have sex once
A year and it's satisfied for a year.
When a man eats, he hungers for more,
When a man has sex, he lusts for more.

"Men are not kinder to their own kind either.
They attempt to control every aspect
Of each other's lives to have an advantage.
They try to control each other's souls too.

"Dear God, what bothers me the most is this:
Forgive me for saying it, they use You.
They have books with contradictory words
And they claim that they are Your own true words.
If those inconsistent words are your words,
Then You are not as mighty as I think.

"I am not trying to demean Your people.
I know You are giving them time to grow
And realize that You created each
One of them as a unique individual
And one can't pour them into the same mold.

"The truest of oneself is only when
One is in communion with one's creator."

As Adem meditated, he saw pleasing
And comforting visions, though he was not
Sure whether they were real or was he dreaming?

At dawn he recalled the way the dervishes
Prayed in the cave of Kalaycik Canyon.
They would say that before the existence
Of time and space, there was nothing but God.
He created this cosmos in a split
Second by uttering His Hallowed Name.
Yet that Name is unknowable by us.
If somebody were to know it, he could
Reshape and recreate this universe.

Traditionally one thousand and one
Chosen names are attributed to Him.
And one of those names might be His true name.

The dervishes would chant attributed
Names of God over and over again.
When they could come closer to the True Name,
The walls of the cave would join them in chanting.

The dervishes would tell the boys, "Listen!
Listen! rocks are testifying the Truth."

When they would report what they had witnessed,
Then adults would say, "Oh, those dervishes.
If they had any power would they live
The way they do? In abject poverty?

They're no more than sorcerers and warlocks.
What you've heard was the echoes of their hymns."

Adem started to chant like the dervishes.
When he recited a befitting name,
He felt vibrations in his whole being.
He slowed down his chanting, and concentrated
On that name over and over again.
The vibration transmitted to the rocks
Now the rocks too were chanting and rocking.

XLVIII. Apparition of Akgelin

Astonishingly Akgelin's statue
Was chanting and dancing counterclockwise.
As the statue danced, a beautiful young
Lady revealed herself in flesh and blood.

She said, "I see that you are not surprised.
Why should you be? We'd known each other during
Our past lives, though I did not look the same.
After all those years, it is the right time
For me to reveal my identity.

"What you know about me through the folk songs
And legends sound as if I am a myth.
Truly legends and myths are moving truths.
They are engraved in people's consciousness.
The conscious is the eye of God in man.

"My name is Alexandrina, the daughter
Of Helenus, the prophet of Troy, and Iris,
The messenger of Zeus, and granddaughter
Of Priam, the King of Troy, and Hecuba,
The mother of Hector and Queen of Troy.

"Just before I was born, on the surface
The kingdom was powerful and prosperous.
However, beneath the surface ill omens
Were lurking for the eyes that could see them.

"When my Uncle Paris was in the womb,
It was prophesied that he'd be the cause
Of the ruination of the kingdom.

So, Paris was exposed at Mt. Ida.
It looked as if disaster was averted.

"Helenus and Iris knew otherwise.
Paris was being reared by the shepherds.
Troy was to be ruined because of him.

"It was my parents' inevitable
Destiny that they should have a daughter.

"Since they knew what was to come over Troy,
They were hesitant to bring forth a child.

"When the Fates challenged my parents, and asked
Why they were not complying with their fate?
My parents presented the hardship that
A child will face in an ominous future,
And tried to extract favors from the Fates.

"Kindly, Clotha spun the thread of my life,
But Lachesis did not measure the length
Of it and Atropos did not cut it.
The Fates said, 'We have no power to grant
Immortality to any mortal,
Yet what we have given is close to it.
Only she'll decide the time of her death.'

"Then my parents pleaded to Proteus,
For me to have the gift of *shape-shifting*,
And their last request was also granted.

"I'm not an immortal as legends say,
But I can live as long as it's called for,
And I can take any shape I desire.

"As a child I lived the life of a princess:
Leisure time for play and time for schooling.
My cousins and I were taught by the best
Teachers of the Royal Gymnasium.

We swam daily in the Scamander River
And on holidays in the Hellespont."

XLIX.   Trojan Wars

Akgelin

After my tenth birthday the war started.
Since the outcome of that war is well known
I'll mention the blows that hurt me the most.

Greeks were honest. They beseeched candidly:
'Oh, Gods high above. Help us. Give us strength
From your strength to burn down the holy Troy,
To slay all Trojan male population,
To enslave their women and girls, and carry
Them by the boat loads to the land of Greeks,
To have Troy's gold and take it back with Helen.'

They've received everything that they prayed for
And also killed the boys yet to be born.
They'd managed to silence all mouths by leaving
Troy behind unlamented and unnoticed.

Hector was a mortal, but he did fight
Like immortals for the defense of Troy.

Achilles was a demigod, but he
Disobeyed the laws of men and the gods.

Patroclus was Achilles' childhood friend,
And his comrade in arms in adulthood.
When he fought with Hector, he was clad in
Achilles' impenetrable armor,
And rode the chariot that was drawn

By the immortal horses of Achilles.
In spite of that, he lost against Hector.

Achilles burned with the fire of revenge.
Killing Hector was not enough for him.
He dragged his body round the walls of Troy,
And wanted to feed it to the dogs.

The most chilling and unforgettable
Experience of my life took place as
I watched the funeral pyre of Patroclus.

Achilles killed numberless sheep and cattle,
Also killed two of Patroclus' nine dogs.
Callously, he slew with swords twelve noble
Trojan youth chosen from among the captives.
Without remorse, he named his murderous
Misdeed as a *sacrifice* to the gods.
But I called that premeditated murder.
When Achilles referred to the Trojan
Victims collectively as *Twelve noble*
Trojan youth, he degraded their selfhood.

They were not collectively twelve noble
Trojan youth; each one of them had his princely
Name, and his individuality.
Those youth can't rest until I name their names:
Acamas Acamides,
Agenor Agenorides,
Ainias Aineiades,
Archeptolemos Archeptolemides,
Chromios Chromiosides,
Daitor Daitorides,
Lycophones Lycophonides,
Melanippos Melanides,
Ophelestes Ophelides,
Ormenos Ormenides,
Orsilocas Orsilochidis and,
Polybos Polybosidis.

I'd not have minded if they were to call
What they'd done as murder, massacre, carnage,
Extermination, or genocide.
But when they apply the word *sacrifice,*
It aggravates me, for it offends God
As well, since the word of *sacrifice* gives
The impression the carnage that is being
Committed is a sacred act to please God.
Why God should be pleased? When He witnesses
A scene where one of His creatures is being
Butchered in His name regardless whether
That living thing is a man or a beast.

Achilles was wounded on his heel, his
Only vulnerable spot, by an arrow
Shot by Paris that caused a mortal wound.

Alas! Human history is not written
With ink, but with blood, always with red blood.

Even under adverse conditions, life
Forces will continue to work for life.

Behind its lofty walls and its brave men,
In Ilium life itself continued,
Though cycle of birth and death were shortened.
The brave young men died too early for Troy,
And the boys grew too fast to take their place.
Cattle, sheep, and men of small towns were killed.

Hector taught me by his own example
That a warrior is not the war maker.
As he battled like immortal heroes,
He always tried to find ways to make peace.

Hector arranged an agreement between
Two warring armies. He had both sides take
A solemn oath that they would watch the duel
Between Paris and King Menelaos;
Compliantly armies would act as seconds,

And the champion would take back Helen,
So the long lasting war will be ended.

However, Hector's plan was not agreeable,
To Hera, nor to the Greek war makers.

Zeus favored the Trojans, but did not use
His will, being afraid of Hera's nagging.
The mighty goddess Hera did not want
The war to stop before Troy was burned down.

The Greek war makers were not satisfied
With less than total destruction of Troy.
Their purpose was not to liberate Helen,
Stop the war, and happily go back home.
Their mission was to gain control over
The Hellespont, and sail through it in peace,
Unchecked and undisturbed by the Trojans,
To reach the Euxine Sea and to the Greek
Colonies at Sinope and Trebizond.
Also to establish new colonies
All along the shores of the Euxine Sea.

During the duel Paris was wounded,
But the victory was not conclusive.
Both sides broke their oaths and the war continued.

The Greeks marched in silence; spoke the same tongue,
But loud cries echoed from the Trojan host,
For they had not one speech since they came from
Many lands to help the Trojans. They were:
Dardanians, Mysians, Carrians,
Daionians, Lelegans, Lycians,
Pelasgians, Phrygians, Thracians,
Amazons, Cilicians and Hittites.

L. The Hittites Came to Help the Trojans

Akgelin

The Hittites and Cilicians arrived towards
The end of the war. They fought as one unit.
Their commander in chief was a dashing
Young Hittite prince, Socos Hittasides.
He looked like a twin brother of Hector
Though he lacked Hector's wisdom and self-control.

He had a charming appeal for girls.
To everyone's surprise, he even charmed
The Amazons into fighting alongside him.

The Hittites had many rare war skills that
Gave them an advantage over their foes.
They had long ago mastered the art of
Smelting iron and forging tempered steel.

While fighting, they wore a steel suit of mail.
Also they covered the vulnerable
Parts of their horses with flexible mail.
Their swords, lances, and shields were made of steel.
The Greek shields, seven layers of ox hide,
Were heavier than Hittite's steel shields.

The Hittites had a rapport with their horses.
Once they mounted their horses, the animal
And the man became one just like a Centaur.

The Hittites did not fight with chariots,
Thus they maintained their flexibility.
Just like an eagle, they would spot their prey,
And with speed ride into battlefield
To get their man, and then swiftly pull back.

They had pure white horses to ride during
Day light, and jet-black ones to ride at night.
It was said that they bred their special breed
Of horses by crossing Egyptian stallions
With mares brought from beyond the Caspian Sea.

They trained those horses on the rocky slopes
Of Mt. Erciyes, plains, and muddy marches
Till the horses grew lithe on any ground.
Before a trainee horse was accepted
As a war-horse, it had to pass the test:
If its rider were to fall it had to stop
For its rider to get back in the saddle;
If its rider were injured or wounded,
Then the horse had to carry its rider
To safety by grabbing its rider's belt.

The Hittite style of warfare: continuous
Attack and retreat and unexpectedly
Attack again was taking its toll and
Turning the war in favor of the Trojans.

LI.   Akgelin and Prince Hittasides

Akgelin

Prince Hittasides was a frequent guest
Of honor at the palace of the King Priam.
Soon Hittasides and I fell in love.
Since the war-weary Trojans were yearning
For any occasion to celebrate,
King Priam and Queen Hecuba gave us
A royal wedding mostly to lift up
The spirits of the Trojan citizens.

Hector was dead and Achilles was dead,
Yet the ten-year-old merciless war was
Continuing, and Troy was standing solid.

The Greeks reassessed their strategy
And, convinced that they could not win the war
In the battlefield alone, and they started
To explore other means to vanquish Troy.

First, the Greeks kidnapped the prophet Helenus
To profit from his gift of prophecy,
Or just to demoralize the Trojans
By denying them his spiritual guidance.

Then they built a colossal wooden horse,
And hid certain Greek chieftains inside it.

All the others struck camp put out to sea,
And hid their ships beyond the nearest island.

On the walls, the Trojan sentries spied
An enormous figure of a horse left
In front of the Scaen Gates. Greeks were gone.

The Trojans were elated for they were
No longer prisoners in their city.
They were free to wander beyond the walls.
They rushed to the sea and to the beaches.

The adults wanted to rediscover
The pleasure and the power of the sea,
And the youngsters enjoyed a completely
New experience by tasting the sea
Water, and feeling the sand under their
Tender feet for the first time in their lives.

What was the significance of the horse?
Most of the people did not care to know.
The flight of the Greeks was enough for them.

The priest Laocoon was frantically urging
The Trojans to destroy the wooden horse.
"I fear the Greeks even when they bear gifts."
He said, and Cassandra echoed his warning.

It was no surprise to Cassandra
That the people would never believe her.
No one listened to what she had to say.

Her gift of prophecy was given by
Apollo when he was in love with her.
However, when Cassandra would not yield
To Apollo's amorous advances,
He was disenchanted. He could not take
Back his gift to her, so he made sure that
No one would believe in her prophecy.

They dragged the horse through the Scaen Gate,
And up to the temple of Athena.

Prince Hittasides pulled back his army
To the foothills of Mt. Ida, in order
To get ready to return to Kanesh.
I stayed at Troy to celebrate the day.
The spirits of the Trojans was high but
Their guards were low. The enemy was cunning.

LII.   Destruction of Troy

Akgelin

During the night the Greek soldiers who were
Hiding in the horse's belly freed themselves.
They flung the gates wide open for the Greek
Host to rush into the sleeping city;
They set fire to the houses, when the puzzled
Trojan soldiers, men and boys emerged from
The burning buildings, the Greeks slaughtered them.

Troy turned into a blazing inferno.
Only the deities could help the Trojans,
And Aphrodite alone came to help.
First, she led her son Aeneas to safety,
Then she removed Helen from the city
And took her to her husband Menelaos.
By the dawn, just two Trojan noblemen
Were alive: Aeneas and Helenus.
Helenus was a captive of the Greeks.

LIII. The Captive Women of Troy

Akgelin

By the morning, all that was left of Troy
Was a band of helpless, captive women:
Their husbands and sons were dead, and their daughters
Were taken from them. They were silently
Waiting for their masters to carry them
Overseas, to degrading slavery.

Demoralized and exhausted, the women
Huddled together like a flock of sheep
Who were surrounded by a pack of wolves.
Except Queen Hecuba who was busy
Tormenting and abusing her captors.
Andromache was standing tall, and trying
To comfort her infant son Astyanax.

The Greek soldiers identified a young
Girl as Queen Hecuba's youngest daughter,
Polyxena, and dragged her from the crowd
And killed her on the grave of Achilles.

Hecuba was drained of her energy,
Subdued, helpless, and appalled by the sight
Of her daughter's decapitated body.
She faced the women and asked, "Who am I?
A gray old lady without any status!
A slave who is driven like cattle?

What misery there is that is not mine?
Country, husband, and children are perished.
Glory of all my family brought low."

And the women answered, "We also stand
At the same point of curse! We too are slaves.

Our girls are crying; call to us with tears:
'Mother, We're all alone in the dark ships,
Now they drive us, and we cannot see you.'"

Hecuba, "My daughters, I can't help you.
Still I feel your misery in my soul.
For the Greeks I am merely a trophy
To exhibit to rouse derisive laughter.
I still can make a statement and can spoil
That demeaning Greek comedy by dying
On the land or the seas of the Trojans."

Queen Hecuba exasperated her
Captors to provoke them to murder her.
Her first wish, to die on the Trojan land
Did not come to pass. They threw her on board.
At an opportune moment, she jumped into
Hellespont, and drowned in the Trojans waters.

Andromache was reasoning, "My son
Is too young to be without a mother.
They will allow me to keep Astyanax."

From the Greek camp a messenger approached
Andromache and mumbled faltering words
And said, "Madam, please do not despise me,
For the news I brought was against my will.
Your son, Astyanax must die—be thrown
Down from the highest battlement of Troy.
Now, now, let it be done. You are a brave
Woman, you must endure. You are alone.
Without Hector—one woman, and a slave.
There is no help coming from anywhere."

She knew what the herald declared was true.
There was no help. She tried to calm her child.
"Weeping, my little one? There, there, you are
Too young to realize what awaits you.
How will it be? Falling down, down all broken,
And none to pity! Kiss me, nevermore.
Come closer, closer. Pass your warmth to me,
When your body grows cold, I will keep your
Warmth in my own body. Bring your breast next
To my chest and let your heartbeats harmonize
With my heartbeats. When your heart beats no more
My heart will continue to beat for yours.
Your mother who bore you—wrap both your arms
Around my neck! Now, kiss me, lips to lips.
Now exhale deep into my lungs, and when
You can breathe no more, I will breath for you.'

The soldiers pulled him from his mother's arms,
And took him away. The last drop of blood
Was drawn with the death of the son of Hector.
The Trojans were thoroughly drained of male blood.

Andromache was given as a prize
Of war to Neoptolemus who killed
The old King Priam at the altar.
He also was the son of Achilles
Who killed her husband Hector, the war hero.
She endured the indignation of fate.
After the death of Neoptolemus,
She married the Trojan prophet Helenus
Who then became the King of Epirus.

After a night of full carnage, the Greeks
Were as tired as the slaughterhouse workers.
Throwing an innocent boy to his death,
As if he were a piece of meat, was much
To bear even for the stone-hearted soldiers.
Reluctantly, without enthusiasm,
They were getting ready to board the women.

LIV. The Hittites, Cilicians and Amazones Saved Some of the Captive Women

Akgelin

The Hittite, Cilician and Amazon
Forces were already at the foothills
Of Mt. Ida preparing to go home.
When they saw that the flames of Troy were lighting
Up the sky, they rushed to investigate.
Their combined forces were ready to fight.

Hittasides was bent on to free me
And as many noble girls as he could.
The Amazons were mainly motivated
With a thirst to take revenge for their Queen
Penthesilea who was killed by Achilles.

Hittasides sent a herald to King
Menelaos with message that his wife
Alexandrina and her twelve maids:
Anastasios, Althea, Alyssa,
Amethyst, Basilia, Calandra,
Calista, Eudora, Geranium,
Gillian, Haidee and Iola
Cannot be considered prizes of war for
By marriage they were now Hittite citizens.

Burned out and homesick Greeks were not willing
To fight once more over a few women.

They released us; the girls who were referred
To as my handmaids were my noble cousins.

LV.   On the Way to Kanesh

Akgelin

Altogether we returned to the camp
At the foothills of Mt. Ida to rest
And to get ready to go back to Kanesh.

The Cillicians and Hittites went on board
At Adramyttium and landed at Lesbos,
Which had the fairest women and weather.
There bodies were healed and spirits were heightened.

With the warm sun, warm beach sands, and warm waters
Of Lesbos, twelve noble ladies opened
Their delicate petals, and bloomed like roses.

The noble soldiers got their scent like bees,
And they were hovering around the maidens
Who were as beautiful as the reflection
Of Aphrodite upon the calm seas.
The men were spreading their five fingers, and greeting
Each other and saying five Ts, which meant
The titillating Trojan team of twelve.

When the soldiers' bodies and minds were healed,
We set sail toward south on calm sea.
When the waves grew choppy and perilous,
We took refuge in the harbor of Smyrna.

The Lydians honored us as their guests,
For they'd a lasting friendship with the Hittites.

Even today, with little search, one can
Find Hittite monuments in Lydia.

The next time, we moored at Halicarnassus
Not that the sea was rough, but the soldiers
And the twelve maidens were dizzy with love.

The Carians welcomed us into their
Homes and temples, and twelve Carian priests
And twelve priestesses performed engagement
Ceremonies, thus twelve maidens and twelve
Noble Hittite soldiers became engaged.

Storms forced us to take refuge at Myra,
And we savored the hospitality
Of the Lycians, and benefited from
Their guidance for the rest of the voyage.

LVI.   Arriving at Cilicia Then Proceeding Toward Kanesh

Akgelin

Under the breezy blue skies and over
The turquoise sea, we sailed east by keeping
The steep Pamphylian coasts to our north.
We disembarked at Soli, and at Tarsus
We said good-bye to our Cilician allies.

With ease we passed the Taurus Mountains through
The Cilician Gates, and not too far
North we could get a glimpse of Mt. Argaeus.

We left behind the warm seas that we loved,
But the sight of Mts. Argaeus and Kartin
Made us feel at home. They looked like the twin
Sisters of Mts. Olympus and Ida.

During his journey to the east, Zeus would
Hold court at the top of Mt. Argaeus.

Through the Tekir Pass, we crossed Mt. Argaeus
And when we descended its north foothills,
We saw both Tubal and Kanesh, which were
Located on a plain that was ringed by hills.

LVII.   The Welcoming Party

Akgelin

Scouts must have spotted us a long ways from
Kanesh and notified King Anitas
And Queen Phrontis of our return from Troy.
When we turned around the bend, a procession
Of townsfolk and armed forces welcomed us.

Socos' brother Kurbanos and his wife
Atthis came forward and they ordered thirteen
Chariots for thirteen couples to ride.
Then Kurbanos pulled back, and let Socos
And me lead the procession toward Kanesh.

The chariot horses were white as snow
And their manes were braided with red ribbons.
Inside, the chariots were decorated
With apricot blossoms and tender thyme.

Once more I realized that the seas,
Olive and fig orchards were left behind,
But I was getting used to the blue skies,
Apricot and pear orchards, and vineyards.

LVIII. Arriving at Kanesh

Akgelin

When we came closer to Kanesh, all I
Could see was an impenetrable wall
Of gray granite which was hiding the city.

We entered the city through Taurus Gate.
At the top of the gate, *the Powerful Mother
Goddess Kubaba* was meditating
And blessings each one of us as we passed.

Lions' statues, on each side of the gate,
Were ready to pounce on any intruder.

Once we were in the city and the iron
Gates were lowered and locked behind us,
We found ourselves in a unique new Word.
There everything was soft and comforting.

All public roads were paved with polished tuff,
And the houses were built with the same stone.
The sidewalks were paved with pinkish marble.
Grapevines were clinging to the city walls
And forming a green veil over the stones.
The air was perfumed by apricot blossoms.

Soon we arrived at the inner citadel.
Its harsh looking walls were unconquerable,
But a veneer of marble softened them.

H. I. Mavioglu

At its gate, we disembarked and entered
The inner royal quarters of Kanesh.

We passed between a row of public buildings.
The palace stood at the top of a mound.
Its walls, columns and domes were built of marble.

An awe-inspiring splendid temple
Was located not too far from the palace.
Mysterious figures and delicate
Flowers were carved on its façade and columns.

Sacred books of the Hittites were inscribed
On the walls in cuneiform characters.

We were led to the reception Hall
Of the palace, and there we were welcomed
To Kanesh, and to the Hittite kingdom
By King Anitas and his Queen Phrontis.

LIX. Welcoming Words of King Anitas

Akgelin

King Anitas said, "I regret that you
Ladies lost your country and your loved ones.
You shed your tear drops into the Aegean
Sea and the Hellespont straight, and their waters
Are purer now due to your added tears.

"I possess no power to change the past,
Nor can I still the echoes of the past,
But I have power to grant you the same
Rights and privileges that every Hittite
Citizen enjoys, and also my Queen
And I will be your surrogate parents.

"I have no power to grant happiness.
It is something you must find in your hearts.

"To honor you, I proclaim the next week
As a national celebration week."

The King Anitas and the Queen Phrontis were
As old as the bones of their ancestors,
And they possessed the wisdom of ages.

LX.   The High Priestess Corina Takes Over

Akgelin

Then the high priestess Corina led us
To the temple and she suggested that
My vows should be renewed to please *Kubaba*,
While other engaged couples would get married.
She added, "To purify your bodies
And recover from the aftereffect
Of ordeals that you had to endure,
For a while you'll stay in the healing spas."

She separated the girls from the men,
And assigned priestesses to both parties.
The spa was a land of milk and honey.
All kind of healthful foods were available,
Save any food that was obtained by killing
A living creature and might hold blood.

Priestess Corina said, "Life lives on life.
When a snake catches a rat, should the snake
Poison its pray and swallow it? Yes, surely.
Should a starved wolf devour a deer? Yes, surely.
Should a man kill a lamb to eat? Maybe.
Should a man kill a lamb as *sacrifice*?
Not at all! He must leave God out of it.

"A man is not like a snake or wolf.
He's been blessed to live on all kinds of foods:

He may choose animal flesh or cereals,
Nutmeats, vegetables, and assorted
Fruits even though they are also alive."

We swam in the hot spring fed, polished pools.
We were massaged daily with chamomile
Shampoo to soften and to smooth our skins.
Priestesses hennaed our fingers and toes
In a way that it left intricate patterns.
They played music to uplift our spirits,
And served barley-ale to cleanse our kidneys.
Bridegrooms were also treated just the same.
Shortly, we felt as if we were reborn.

We were expecting that at any moment
Priestesses were going to start to preach
Without stopping, but that never happened.
We learned the reason when the High Priestess
Corina said, "The body is the temple
Of One, and the soul is a part of One.
When the body is sound and soul is pure,
They will know on their own who is their Source."

They summoned the seamstresses and tailors
To design rare wedding gowns for the brides,
And wedding caftans for the bridegrooms.
The fingers of the brides and bridegrooms were
Sized by the jewelers for the wedding rings.

Within a week all necessary tasks,
For the wedding ceremony, were finished.
Brides' gowns and veils were made of pure white silk,
They were embroidered with purple threads.
Bridegrooms' caftans were made of purple silk,
And were embroidered with white silk threads.

Bridegrooms' parents acted as our parents.
They were standing around the temple threshold.
As we passed them to enter, mothers hung
Double strands of gold coins and pearls around

The necks of the brides, and fathers hung turquoise
Talismans around the necks of bridegrooms
To protect them against the evil eye.

The temple was decorated with flowers
And perfumed with the attar of wild rose.

LXI.   The Wedding Ceremony

Akgelin

Corina called the couples to the altar:
Alexandrina and Socos,
Anastasios and Eurygyus,
Althea and Anatole,
Alyssa and Eunominus,
Amethyst and Damas,
Basilia and Ecrytus,
Calandra and Balthsar,
Calista and Barbabas,
Eudora and Charaxus.
Geranium and Phaon,
Gillian and Longinus,
Haidee and Pittacus, and
Iola and Pelegon

She continued with the ceremony.
"We are here in this temple not to preach,
But to bless the weddings of these young couples.

"All of you are blessed with the gift of love,
So that you could come here to stand as two
And go out with two bodies yet as one.

"Surely there is no mystery to life,
For life treats us just the same whether,
We may be rich or poor, meek or mighty.

"Love is the essence of any union.
It is understood that these young couples
Promised to love and cherish each other
Before they entered into this temple.
What else they could pledge that is eternal?
Youthfulness and beauty are ephemeral,
But love is ageless and everlasting.
The more it's given the more it will thrive.

"Man's power is the foam upon the seas,
But love holds the power of the oceans.

"Passion is the grass fire that fizzles out,
While love harbors the primordial fire.

"In no time your wealth may evaporate,
And your hale health may deteriorate,
But love lets you cope with adversities.

"We are born through a union of a couple,
Since without that union neither a woman
Nor a man is a whole to bring forth life.
Thus marriage is a sacred design
To make man and woman one complete whole.
How could anyone take marriage lightly?

"Marriage is not just a private affair:
It's a covenant between you and God,
It's a contract between you and your neighbors
That you're coming into each other's life
To brighten your days and shorten your nights,
To bring forth children to raise them to be
Sweet and strong, and to know you don't own them,
But you prime them to get out of your house
For them to grasp the meaning of freedom.

"The pillars of this temple stand apart
To support the weight of the massive dome.
You must not lean on each other, yet stand
Close enough to support your family.

Look at the fruitful trees of the orchard,
They don't grow under each other's shade.

"Respect for each other's integrity,
Since an alloy of two noble metals
Is much stronger than either one of them.
And a strong rope is but flimsy hemp fibers
Twined together to strengthen each other.

"A wise farmer will not hitch an ox with
A water buffalo to form a team,
Knowing the buffalo will overpower
Any strong ox and the team will be weakened.

"Attempting to establish dominance
In a marriage is like letting strong acid
Drip on the foundation of your dwelling,
And waiting to see when it will collapse."

She asked us to exchange our wedding rings,
And chanted a hymn from the holly tablets.

Those marriages were the rebirth of Kayserians.
Each couple was blessed with six boys and girls.
This blessing continued in their descendants
Until every newborn Kayserian
Child was infused with Trojan blood and genes.
Even today it's shown in their keenness.

After the ceremony, we were led
To the reception hall for celebration.

All of us settled down and felt at home.
We slowly learned the Hittite ways without
Being forced into them. Happy we were.

Shortly after my arrival I gave
Birth to my twins, and in due time the other
Couples were also blessed with healthy babies.

LXII.   The Death of the King Anitas and the Struggle Between Princes

Akgelin

King Anitas' health was deteriorating,
And Socos and his brother Kurbanos
Were campaigning hard to be the next king.
The military forces were for Socos,
And the civilians were for Kurbanos.

Kurbanos was a man of common sense
And a capable administrator,
Besides, he was willing to share the power.

Socos was after absolute power.
Even his concept of love was ownership.
What he could not own he'd rather destroy.

King Anitas died not too long after
My twins had their first birthday celebration.

Since King Anitas ruled and lived so long
To his subjects he was both a wise King
And a father figure they'd ever known.

The people from this kingdom, and the head
Of states from all around the world came
To Kanesh to pay their final respects.

Corina delivered the eulogy,
"We are assembled here in this temple
To say farewell to a man who finished
One short leg of his journey on this Earth.

"When a man dies, he leaves all his possessions
And titles behind. This body that lies
Here is no longer a king, for he left
His kingdom behind for us to look after.
If he were a pauper, he could not leave
Anything more or less than a still body.

"To give back what is borrowed from the soil,
The body shall surely turn into dust,
Although the soul shall return to the One.

"The One is the sole source of this universe.
Since He is unknowable to us mortals,
We think of Him within human conceptions.
Even the *Mother Goddess Kubaba*
Is a shadow puppet who's put to motion
By the One's light, which shines behind the veil.

"God alone shall pass judgment on the soul's
Effectiveness, and its integrity
While it was tutoring the Self on this Earth.
If He is pleased with the Soul's performance,
Then He will allow that Soul to merge with
Himself to form an *Eternal Union*.
If not, Soul will be sent back to the Earth.

"Any question as to what happens after
The Union is a vain curiosity,
For *the Union* is the ultimate blessing.

"The One does not operate an Elysian
Fields to entertain the returning souls,
Nor does He run a Hades to hurt them.
Since the universe is a part of Him,
He has no place to locate a Hades.

"We've no authority to talk about
The spiritual life of any man.
It's an issue between him and his God.
Still we must talk about his relationship
With other men while he was among them.

"We hesitate to pass a quick judgment
On a deceased, yet whatever we might
Say about his conduct becomes a judgment.
And that judgment will remains as a code
Of ethics for future generations.

"If a man had ample worldly possessions,
We ask how did he manage that fortune?
How much did he spend for the care of poor?

"If a man had political power,
We ask how did he apply that power?
To oppress or to empower people?

"If a man had intellectual power,
We ask, did he exercise that power
To spread wisdom or to glorify himself?

"If a man were poor with worldly possessions,
We ask, did he apply the nobleness
Of his heart to feel the pains of others?

"King Anitas used his power justly.
He uplifted his subjects when he could,
If he could not, then he felt their sufferings.

"We don't have any claims against his soul.
May his soul merge with the Keeper of Souls."

LXIII. The End of Kanesh and Alexandrina's Shape-Changing

Akgelin

In accord with Hittite laws, upon the death
Of a ruling king, the grand vizier would
Become an acting king for forty days.
The next king would be elected among
Eligible princes during this time.

Socos had no chance to become the King.
Because of his arrogant behavior,
He even lost the support of armed forces.

It was prognosticated by Cassandra
And Helenus that the end of Kanesh
Would come through fire, but the lives would be spared.

I could not live through one more disaster.
So I took my twins and slipped out of Kanesh.
I stayed a few days with the Assyrians
Who were living beyond the city walls.
When the soldiers started to search for me,
I left the Assyrian settlement,
For if I were to be found among them,
Socos would've inflicted harm on my hosts.

I came to this caldera, but the soldiers
Were just behind me. Being trapped, my only
Viable option was *to change our shapes.*

It would've been easy to change into birds,
But the archers' bows were tight to shoot us;
Instead, I chose to turn us into stones.
The soldiers stood aghast before leaving..

Then we reemerged from our shielding shells,
Then I notice that Kanesh was ablaze.
All the marble buildings and sidewalks added
Fuel to the inferno of the city.
The people of Kanesh moved to Tubal,
With my twins I joined them to live our lives.

I left our statue in the caldera
To let the refreshing spring rains bathe it,
The rays of summer sun to warm its core,
And the winter snow to blanket it snugly.

LXIV.   A Turkish Lady Comes upon Alexandrina's Statue

Akgelin

When the pioneering Turkish shepherds
Came to the highlands of Mt. Erciyes,
They knew less about the land than their sheep.
As they grazed their flocks, they were searching for
The next alpine meadow with greener grass.
A young mother with her daughter and son
Unexpectedly came upon my statue.

Although it was not alive, they were glad
To find a human image in the wilds.
The mother named me: *Akgelin (White Bride),*
The daughter named my daughter *Sari Cigdem
(Yellow Crocus),* and the little son named
My son *Mavi Sumbul (Blue Hyacinth.)*

The next day, they came back together with
Their friends to visit. They were in a festive
Mood, wearing their best flowery costumes,
And they were bearing gifts of white roses,
Yellow crocuses and blue hyacinths.
Ever since they've kept the same tradition.

I held dear my given name, *Akgelin,*
For it gave me a new identity,
And a feeling of being accepted.

LXV.   Perplexing Powers

Akgelin

1. Veiled Visions

Adem, just like most mortals, you possess
No vivid memories of your past lives.
Before I talk more about your past lives
I will remind you of an incident
That happened during your present life.

You'd a vision when you were a young man,
But you told about it to no one being
Afraid that the people might think that what
You had seen was an hallucination.

You were in the Ademoglu Mosque standing
In the last row behind the prayer nave
And holding up a rolled up parchment scroll.
Your grandmother, Elmas, was standing on
Your right side and praying devotedly,
And in her prayers mentioning your name.
On your left side a young lady was standing
Who was familiar to you, yet you were
Not sure of her real identity.
Now lift your eyes and look at my face.
Now you know the truth. I'm the lady who
Was standing on your left side in that mosque.

You unfurled the scroll, but its back was blank
And you did not know what was written on
The side that was facing the congregation.

When the hodja noticed the scroll, he broke
His prayer and slowly approached the scroll.
He paid his utmost respect to the scroll,
And the rest of the prayers followed suit.

You were sure that you had nothing to do
With what might have been written on the scroll.
You happened to be merely holding it.

You knew that you could have opened fire on
The praying faithful, or set the whole mosque
On fire, yet they would not break their worship.
To this day, you still wonder about what was
Written on the scroll that made it so holy.

In real life you knew the hodja of
The Ademoglu Mosque, Nuh Imamoglu,
And most of the devoted who were there.
Even though the congregation that you
Had seen appeared neighborly, you could not
Be sure as to where and when you met them.

After giving you this information,
I will now shed some light on your vision.
The hodja was the spirits of prophets,
And the prayers were the spirits of saints.
On the scroll the True Name of God was written.
That was the reason they interrupted
Their worship, for nothing less would they ever
Pay any attention much less to pause.
They were silent according to the saying:
'Those who know don't talk. Those who talk don't know.'

Even though we were allowed to be there,
Still the Sacred Name was not shown to us

For we did not have the maturity
To be privy to such an Awesome Power.

2. Implied Intuitions

While you and your family were living
At Tucson, Arizona, your house was
Located, in a new subdivision,
At the Santa Catalina foothills.
Everyone's backyard was contiguous
With high desert, which supported a large
Variety of stunted shrubs and cacti.
Your three-year-old son was found of cacti.
He began to speak by learning the common,
And also botanical names of cacti.

He would slip out of the house with your German
Shepherd to wander into the desert,
And then he would return with a cactus.
Usually it was not a big problem.
Gale would call the dog, and he would lead her
To your son and she would bring your son home.

In the mornings you would take the highway
Straight to your office, but in the evenings
When you'd come to the junction, without thinking,
You'd take the short cut, or the scenic route,
Which would overshoot your house by three miles
To the north, and then you had to drive three
Miles extra to the south to arrive home:
No profound or involved decision making.

One evening you were working overtime,
And trying to decide as to which road
To take before you came to the junction.
'Take the shortcut you are already late.
No, take the scenic-route you need diversion.'
Finally you took the scenic-route. So what?
You have done that many a time before.

There was nothing new, same old paloverdes,
Mesquites and saguaros were casting long
Shadows under the setting desert sun.
When you reached Ina Road at dusk you had
To slow down, it was congested and many
Cars were parked on the both shoulders of the road.
Then with your peripheral vision you
Saw only the tail of your dog and you
Called, Thumper, your dog and your son came out
Of the bushes and jumped into your car.
You made eye contact with a young lady
In a blue Volkswagen bug. She was I.
When you arrived home, Gale was in panic,
And on the phone trying to reach the sheriff.

You called that occurrence a coincidence,
Yet you knew statistically it was not
Feasible, for you to be there where you
Were needed at that precise split second.

There are many variables to do
A valid statistical analysis.
You might not have taken the scenic-route,
You could have been stuck in heavy traffic
And missed the right moment to locate them,
Or you could have driven fast and passed them.

What led you there was your intuition.
Intuition is a way for the people
To connect with their own souls, and the soul
Is always connected with other souls.

LXVI.   From the Beginning to the End

Akgelin

1. Myths

I have seen several faiths come and go,
But as they went, they left their myths behind.
So the myths continue to thrive by changing
Their colors without changing their essence.

Old Greek, Babylonian, Assyrian,
Egyptian, Hittite, Hindu, and Hebrew
Myths are intricately woven into
Major religions of the present age.
Underlying psychology is simple:
Promise them dancing damsels of Heaven,
Or scare them with eternal fires of Hell.

2. Man Believes According to his Spiritual Development

I have seen many prophets come and go.
All of them must have received the same message.
It had to be the same, for there is one Source.
I have heard them giving the same Good News:
"Love each other and hold all life forms dear."

If that is the fact, why are there so many
Distinct religions, and so many sects?
At a given time, men can believe in
And can perceive according to the level
Of their spiritual maturity.

When the Earth was thought to be the exact
Center of the fathomless universe:
The sun was a fiery rock to supply
Heat and shed light upon the mother Earth.
The stars were the ornaments on the dome,
The Mediterranean was the great sea,
And the Euphrates was the great river.
That world needed a benevolent Owner
To run it to benefit the people.
He was all powerful, just, and loving.
He could do no wrong, yet there was discord.

In defense of God, they propose that evil
And wickedness are caused by the Devil,
And it is beyond the control of God.
There is a dichotomy in that logic.
Why an omnipotent and loving God
Won't render null and void that Evil Force?
Is He incapable of doing so?
Or is He willingly allowing that Foul
Force to corrupt His innocent people?

3. Prophets and Organizers

A prophet is not a fit organizer.
His idea of love is universal,
Although people are partial to loving
Their own much more than loving their neighbors.
They want to be served first in love and goods.
This selfishness invites the organizers
To take charge to give vantage to their people.
Once the organizers begin to swaddle

The New Revelation in the layers
Of rituals, rites, and foreign languages
The Good News is smothered to death and buried.

Today's mosques, churches, and synagogues stand
On different foundations that were laid
By the organizers not by the prophets.

Jesus instilled unconditional love
And unconditional nonviolence,
But the crusaders, so-called followers
Of Jesus, on their way to Jerusalem,
Blazed a trail of treachery and torture.
When they reached Jerusalem, they massacred
That city's Jewish and Muslim citizens.

That day, Jesus came down to Jerusalem
As he wept for the innocent victims,
He blessed the souls of the slain Jews and Muslims.
Even under those ungodly conditions,
Jesus' love would not allow him to curse
The killers—he prayed for their forgiveness.

The crusaders justified their offenses
By saying that the slain were infidels,
Consequently, they did not possess souls.

4. Religious Persecution

When a new religion is established
Its members had to endure a period
Of persecution. Paradoxically,
During that trying period members
Hold on tight to love and nonviolence.
When the militants gain power, they teach
People how to use the strength of the sword,
And in turn they become the persecutors.

Lucky for the Christians, their period
Of persecution lasted for centuries,
So the concept of unconditional
Love and nonviolence could take root.
When they could get rid of the militant
Faction they could uphold the basic doctrines.

On the way of their evolution Christians
Passed through a period of sectarian
Conflicts that brought on dreadful fratricide.
Then they called on brotherly love to cleanse
Their souls; and in turn brother embraced brother.

Mohammed was given the revelation
Of lasting love, compassion and tolerance.
As it had been the case with other faiths,
He and his followers were persecuted.
But their persecution did not last long.
The organizers found the sword too soon.
Then the militant factions took over.
They veiled the compassion and tolerance,
Which led to wiping-out the ancient scrolls
Of the Library of Alexandria.

5. Conflicts Between the Clerics and the Heads of States

All through human history the most crushing
Conflicts for the people had been the conflicts
Between the clerics and the heads of states.
When these two monster fight with each other,
Innocent human beings are tormented.

For the salvation of the common people,
Christians disengaged the church from the state
And gave each one a domain to rule over.
Ever since conflict was resolved, in their
Ways, the church and the state are helping people.

6. Male Organizers and Women

From the beginning, male organizers
Were conspiring to have the upper hand
On another group of human beings.
They found this group quickly for they were living
With them: their mothers, their wives and their daughters.

They concocted a myth about Adam's
Rib and Eve…the snake and Eve, and the apple.
There, they found a divine decree declaring
That the woman is made of a man's spare part
And she's deceitful, thus less than a man.

Only recently Christian and Jewish
Women have gained equality with men,
Therefore, their integrity is restored.
Yet their Muslim sisters are still suffering.

7. Is God a Puppet in the Hands of Organizers?

According to the organizers God
Was in their corner, and He'd do whatever
The organizers wanted Him to do.

Hebrews were quick to single out themselves
As the only Chosen People of God.
If God were on their side who could hurt them?
But their claim caused resentment among other
Nations and they persecuted the Jews.

There was a good reason for people to think
That God would favor them over others,
For their God was like a national God.
Why should He have any love or concern
For the cosmos? which was unknown to them.

8. *Women in an Islamic Society*

In a society that was practicing
Infanticide among their female infants,
Mohammed much improved the female's fate.
In those days women went around bare-breasted.
He said, "The women should cover their breasts.
Besides, both sexes should dress modestly."
Knowing that for the modesty of Eve
A single fig leaf was modest enough;
He did not pass a dress code on the women.

The organizers did not want to leave
The issue of modesty to the women.
They designed a big black bag for the women.
They have kept them in it for centuries.
Why change the style? It is cheap to purchase.
A black bag for each woman in all seasons.

If it were an issue of women's clothing,
I would not bother to talk about it.
The issue is not about fashion,
But it is all about losing control
Over their own bodies and affairs.

The Quran did not stipulate that woman
Must be secluded and isolated.
Yet organizers did that not only
In the mosque but also in daily life.

Just recently, a Muslim Queen was not
Allowed to attend her husband's funeral.

When a military Muslim faction
Took control over their Islamic
Brothers, after a long bloody warfare,
Promptly, they forgot all about forgiveness.
Their first administrative achievement
Was to sort out the souls in line with sex.
The female physicians and female nurses

Were forbidden to practice medicine.
Public school doors were shut in the girls' faces.
By denying learning to females,
They committed the worst crime against man.

9. I Have Learnt From the Wise and From the Wisecrackers

All through millennia, I've learnt from
The wise as well as from the wisecrackers.
I am impressed only with a few people:

With Haci Bektas for saying, "Practicing
Any religion in any language
Other than one's mother language is not
A faith but an imitation of faith."

With Hunat Hatun for her being close
To her roots and for having a free spirit.

With Agop Bagciyan who was a Christian.
He was playing cards with Osmanoglu
And Aslanoglu who were Muslim Turks.
Osmanoglu said, "Agop we have been
Bosom buddies and brothers since childhood.
Only our faiths pull a veil between us.
Why don't you become a Muslim like us."
Agop answered, "I have thought about that.
If I could be a faithful Muslim like
Imamoglu, I would've become a Muslim,
But I don't have the spiritual
Fortitude and faith of Imamoglu.
At best I can be a Muslim like you.
I'd still gamble, drink and chase girls."

10. There Is One God

In Islamic Faith there is no doubt or
Compromise about the Oneness of God.
When Mohammed died people were perplexed.
But the first caliph, Abu Bakr, praised the truth
By saying, "Those of you who were worshipping
Mohammed must believe that he is dead.
Those of you who were worshiping God must
Trust that He is eternal and alive."

There is a total tolerance and acceptance:
"Those who believe (in the Quran)
And those who follow the Jewish (scriptures),
And the Christians and the Sabians,—
Any who believe in God
And the Last Day,
And work righteousness,
Shall have their reward
With their Lord: On them
Shall be no fear, nor shall they grieve." [1]

And the Quran shows the end of our journey:
"(We seek) Thy forgiveness,
Our Lord, and to Thee
Is the end of all Journeys." [2]

What an excellent end for any journey!
For it won't end in Hell or in Heaven.

Islam is a religion of One God
Filled with love, mercy, acceptance and peace.
Since it's younger, it groans with growing pains.

---

[1] Quran, 2/62,
[2] Quran, 2/285

11. Jihad

The Islamic militants are still strong.
They have made the sword a religious symbol.
Some nations display the sword on their flags.
The preachers sport a sword as they go up
To the pulpit to preach about the peace.

They still have the cryptic word of jihad.
For the faithful, jihad is an inward
Journey to enlighten one's inner space.
For the militants, jihad is a war,
So-called holy war against unbelievers.
How can a faith rate any war as holy?

These military factions try to enforce
The ritualistic rules of the faith,
Which are the outer shells of the religion,
But they don't stand for the soul of the faith.

12. Symbiotic Alliance of the State and Religion

Mostly there is no clear-cut separation
Between religious concerns and the state.
They formed a symbiotic alliance
To perpetuate their oppressive powers.

Since people have both a Soul and a Self,
Since they need different kinds of nurturing,
They must have two sources to obtain them.

No form of government can instill faith
In the hearts of men, but by force it
Can enforce the ritualistic rules
To maintain the outer shell of religion.
Without being concerned whether its inside
Is viable and thriving or rotten.

One Islamic kingdom is practicing
This system so the king can keep his throne,
And his clan can suck the blood of the kingdom.

13. Warped Sense of Justice

By no means, is it the fault of Islam,
Yet the Muslims have a warped sense of justice.
They do not hesitate to cut the hand
Of a man for stealing a loaf of bread.
They also do not mind to look the other
Way while a corrupt official steals millions.

There is nothing new about corruption.
Great poet Fuzuli wrote long ago,
"I went to a government office and said
Shalom but no one bothered to take it,
Because what I offered was not a bribe."

14. Why Muslims Can't Achieve the Greatness of the Past?

Muslims look into their past achievements
In algebra, algorithm, architecture,
Astronomy, medicine, chemistry
Commerce, poetry and other areas
That human mind and spirit can accomplish
And they ask, what has happened? Why not now?

Their kings, dictators and fundamentalists
Won't say: you have no political freedom,
No economic or religious freedom,
You keep half the work force locked inside during
Business hours just to while away their days.

They won't say, Islam commands you to search
And discover new scientific knowledge,
Or absorb it wherever you find it.

They won't honestly say, our primary
Concern is to control your mind in order
To maintain stagnation and status quo.

They won't say, Quran is a guide to man.
To benefit from it you must grasp it.
Memorizing it in a foreign language,
Like a parrot, won't help without knowing
The meaning of it in your mother language.

They won't say, we founded a technophobic
World to live in, and we condemn all new
Findings as the invention of infidels.
That way we let the Ottoman Empire
Lag one step at a time into its coffin.

Instead they say to their citizenry:
We feel sorry about your poverty
But we can't do anything about it,
For our hands are tied by the superpowers.

Since people can't criticize their rulers
Or their religious leaders, they project
Their resentments to the external forces.

15. The Ottoman Tolerance and the Secular Republic of Turkiye.

Since the Ottoman Empire was composed
Of many nations with many religions,
The Turks learned acceptance and tolerance.
They've been living under a secular
Form of state for over four generations.
But secularism is still under siege
From external and internal intrigue.

After all these years religious militants
Are trying to get rid of the secular
Form of government, and still conspiring
To bring theocracy into Turkiye.

Yet today's secular government has
A ministry of religious affairs,
And supporting religious education.
This reluctant relationship between
The government and religion is causing
Discontentment among the citizens.

Soon Turkiye will have the will to take
The last step and will cut the umbilical
Cord between the government and religion,
So that each can grow healthy separately,
And nurture the citizens whom they serve.
Always the will of God shall come to pass.

LXVII.   Spiritual Evolution

Akgelin

Since ancient times the men have been evolving.
Today nobody ever justifies
Human sacrifice under any guise,
Yet the animal sacrifice continues.
Furthermore, the evolution of men
Did not reach a level to consider
That war is a mass crime of the ancients.
Thankfully, the rules of war have evolved.
No longer is the winner free to act
With uncontrolled vengeance and take the lives
And properties of the vanquished people.

Now there is an idea of *War Crimes*.
Though it is too hard to prove and too slow
To serve justice, and make restitution,
It is still a reassuring concept.

We developed weapons of mass destruction,
But we have the resolve not to use them.

Ethnic uprising and ethnic cleansing
Continues, and they're the worst of conflicts,
For the fight is between friends and neighbors
Who have lived together for centuries.
They mixed blood with each other and grew kin.
They had shed their blood together to save
The land that they're now trying to divide
Where a border cannot pull them apart.

Most of the men are already evolved
To a level where they're willing to give
Room for each other to grow together.

Another good news for the Earth's peoples
Is the notion of *basic human rights*:
When it is implemented, a person
Shall be a person in order to reach
His or her full potentials on the basis
Of his/her spiritual and mental mettle.

A person shall not be classified or
Pulled back on the basis of his or her
Race, religion or nationality.

Still Islamic organizers are trying
To keep the status quo by enforcing
The Islamic dress custom on women.
They are not interested in women's
Spiritual and mental ascension,
Or their economic independence:
Keep them under the cover and hidden;
By coaxing they are getting girls to say,
"I've a right not to use my God given rights."

LXVIII. Freedom of Thought

Akgelin

Without the freedom of thought there's no light,
And only truth is the ultimate truth.
At the end of our journeys, we will find
The Truth, why not search and find it sooner?

Recently an Islamic country was
Offended by the writings of an author.
At one time, the people of that country
Gave birth to freethinking sages and poets.
Even to this day, that country is blessed
With capable writers with the brains who can
Refute the ideas of that author.

Instead the imams chose to take the sword
To silence the author with brute force.

LXIX. Prophecies

Akgelin

1. Kayserian Youth

The spirit of Hunat Hatun is alive.
Right now many Kayserian girls are
Inheriting her spirit and they shall
Continue to inherit in the future.
In turn, these freethinking and upright girls
Shall infuse new life into Kayserians.

They shall bring an end to superstition
By overcoming ignorance and sloth.
They shall expose and nullify all form
Of oppression over the minds of beings.
They shall overcome social tyranny
For it penetrates much more deeply into
The details of life to enslave the souls
By its prevailing opinions and feelings.

They shall read the scripture in their own tongue,
And find the truth hidden between the words.
They shall listen to the eternal message
Of God, which has no beginning, no end.
They shall come to know that their religion
Is known to their God and themselves alone.

It shall be hard, for no one will help them.
They'll say, "Are you listening to the Devil?
Here is the scripture. It's the word of God.
Who do you think you are? How dare you to
Use your own measuring stick to measure?"
Still they shall do alone what they must do.
They shall be encouraged, knowing they can
Be right without convincing anyone.

They shall delight in the things of the mind:
Love and beauty, kindness and tender feelings.
Kayserians shall rise to the highest
Level of spiritual evolution.
Their hearts shall be filled with eternal love.
Negative energies shall disappear,
For there shall be no room in their hearts for
Fear, hate, envy, jealousy, and prejudice.
They shall purge egotism out of their
Hearts and replace it with altruism.
People shall not judge each other, but find
Each other through the path between their hearts.

2. The End of the Earth

The sun shall grow cold and the Earth shall shiver
Under the layers of stratified ice.
Then Mt. Erciyes shall open its vents
Into the center of the Earth to tap
Its reserved energy to create
A microclimate for Kayseri to last.
When the Earth's energy is exhausted,
Then Mt. Erciyes shall consume itself
To generate energy for Kayseri.

Finally the Sun shall collapse on itself
To consume itself and its satellites
In a split second to end its life cycle.

What'll be missed in the Universe? Nothing!
What'll be perished from the Cosmos? Nothing!
A new star shall be born, shall live and die.
The life forces shall continue to work
To bring forth new lives to thrive and to die.

3. I Shall Miss the Mother Earth

I feel sad about the fate of the Earth,
Although I can do nothing to change it.
In this unfathomable Universe
There are and there shall be life-giving planets
But there shall be no other place like Earth.

No other planet shall have the right distance
From its sun to have the variety
Of seasons to renew its vitality.
Among the seasons I shall miss the spring
And its blue crocus blooming at the edge
Of a melting snow patch to give new hope.
I shall miss bleeding heart and baby's breath.

No other planet shall have its moon nearby
To stir its oceans to keep them alive.
I shall not miss the power of the moon
But its cool light to brighten my dark nights.

I shall long for the Earth from her North Pole
To frozen continent of Antarctica;
From her abyssal plains to Mt. Everest,
From her Sahara Desert to rain forests.
I shall miss the oases and their palms
And the naked hills with their scent of sage.

I shall miss the Earth from her one-cell "grass"
Of her oceans to the giant sequoia.

I shall miss the Earth from her animals
The size of a pinhead to her great whales.

I shall miss the beaches with its gentle
Waves lapping my legs; its shifting sands
Tickling my feet to show its playfulness.

I shall miss the ruby-throated hummingbird
Also the ocean going albatross.

I shall miss the quietude of the night
And blue jay breaking it with its dawn song.

I shall miss the most newborn snow-white lambs
Suckling their mothers in a green pasture,
And the newborn babies suckling their mothers.

Akgelin stopped talking and the *Eternal
Moment* rained with its absolute silence.
Then she said, "I've been spending time as though
There is no end to it. I must now be leaving.
Time is on no one's side; don't count on time."

LXX.   All Past Lives of Adem Are Revealed

Adem stirred but the time was distorted.
He could not judge how long he was blessed with
The presence and counsel of Akgelin:
Maybe a minute, Or a millennium?

To clear his head at the cool mountain breeze,
He climbed to the northern rim of the hollow,
And sat at the edge of the cliff to look
Over the boundless countryside below.
There *the veil of time lifted and the circle
Of time* descended in front of his eyes.
The past, the present, and the future
Came to focus at an *Eternal Moment*.
The past replayed itself as it had happened,
And the veil of uncertainty is lifted
From the face of the featureless future.
He started to live his past lives as they
Had happened, and reported to himself.

1. The Beginning Before the Beginning

I am in a place that is not a place.
There is no here and there, no up or down.
There is no left and right, no right or wrong.
I am in a time that is not a time.
There, there is neither before nor after,
No getting ahead, no falling behind,
There is no gender, no male, no female.
Yet I am in bliss for I am with Him.

H. I. Mavioglu

One day that was neither daylight nor night,
He pronounced His true name, and with the fire
Of that Word nonexistence turned into
The existence, which we call the Cosmos.

All things became an insignificant
Part of God, but no part became God Himself.

The beginning and the end came into
Reality with existence, and time
Began to mark the end of the beginning.
Prior to the existence of matter
And space there was no beginning, no end.
When I heard the Word, I split from Him as
A soul, yet I was still a part of Him,
For I had no form to come between us.

I watched stars to take their place in space,
And pay their respect to each other's space.

Since I had no body to hinder me,
I could squeeze into any place or thing,
Without being crushed to death or imprisoned.
I could not be burnt in intense heat,
And could not be frozen in extreme cold.

Still in that vast universe, I felt lost
And searched for an alive place to anchor.

I watched the Earth as she kept her doors open
To the cosmic forces to capture life
Giving things to acquire life for herself,
To give life to all other living things.

The Earth's magnetic field became her soul,
Which guided her and held all things together.
The Earth cooled just enough to form the land
And filled most of the land with the oceans.

The Earth used the gravitational force
Of the Moon to give rhythm to the oceans.
She dilated her pores at the bottom
Of the oceans to supply energy
To warm the water of oceans to turn
Them into the fertile womb of herself.

Life forces acquired a form in that womb.
Then living things got hold on the land.
The Earth acquired an atmosphere all around.

Ancestors of the vegetation worked
Day and night to manufacture oxygen
And atmosphere became the lungs of Earth.

2. Body and Brain Organism that Is Called Self

I, the soul, wished to have a brain and body
Organism with psychological and
Biological needs to share its life.
I called this mortal organism the Self.
The Self came into being with demands
To sustain its temporary life form.

I, the Soul, wished to be an integral
Part of the Self by giving all I have,
But the Self could not hold my energy.
If I were to shift all my energy
Into the Self, it would have exploded.
Yet a fraction of my Soul's energy
Puts the substance of God into the Self.

I was not created in the image
And likeness of God, for God has no shape.

As the Earth changed her shape to renew herself,
I also changed my shape several times,
And each time, I looked into my reflection
In the water, I was satisfied only

When my reflection showed a human face.
My having a shape did not distanced me
From God, for His substance is in my Soul.

3. I Am the People

My Self's needs partly tied me to the Earth.
I multiplied and I called them the people.
I'm the sire of the oldest living being
And the child of the youngest living being.

Initially the self was contented
With its daily bread; then it increased its
Demands, and used me for its purposes.
Shall I ever learn to prosper the Self
Without slaying the Soul in the process?

Mt. Erciyes was still young and fiery.
She was wearing a glowing crown and rippling
Red ribbons which were flowing down over
The skirt to form a backbone for the land.

At times she would grow angry, and would puff
Her heavy breath which would condense and come
Down to form a new skin for the young land.
Also it would smother, under its weight,
Living things that were trying hard to thrive.

Before long, dormant seeds of life would sprout,
Even with much more vigor than before.
In due time Mt. Erciyes grew much wiser,
And covered her old head with a white scarf.
Since then she has never taken it off.

Mt. Erciyes leads a modest lifestyle.
She keeps herself half-nude to channel her
Life giving water into the aquifers,
And then lets them percolate as springs,
Thus the fields could clothe themselves in green furs.

4. I Am an Anatolian

I am still the people, yet I began
To call myself an Anatolian,
And I started to speak Anatolian,
Which became the root language for the rest
Of the Indo-European Languages.

I was the farmer. I labored shoulder
To shoulder with my stout oxen on my
Rocky fields to grow golden-headed wheat.
I was the baker, and I baked the bread.
I fed my children, only then I rested.

I built villages to shelter my body,
But I founded Kayseri as a city
To comfort and to nurture my spirit.
I adorned it with temples, and I honored
The temples with many gods and goddesses.
The faithful worshiped only the ones who
Had the power to condemn them to Hades
Or to reward them with Elysian Fields.
For the rest of the gods and goddesses,
They sang and danced during their holy days.

I worshipped One God who had no image,
Yet touched everything in the universe.

I took care of my vineyards on the sunny
Side of the slopes to grow ruby red grapes.
I was the wine maker, also the priest.
To please the gods, I offered my best wine.
I raised the rose and extracted its attar
To perfume my pretty temple priestesses.
I was the bard, I wrote the hymns and chanted
Them to please the gods, and to charm the folks.

I was hard on myself. I wished to hold
Perfection and the ultimate truth.
When I was intoxicated with pride,

I thought I possessed both of them in me.
When I grew sober, I realized that
Attainment of perfection and unfolding
The truth is a privilege, not a right.

I was a sinner, for I amassed knowledge
Without benefiting from my knowledge.
I pursued science for its sake without
Thinking how it would affect the people.

When I was poor, I grew needy and jealous.
My view of wealth warped, since I did not see
The generosity of the heart as wealth.

When I was rich, I scorned work, pursued pleasure,
And grew into a keeper of my wealth.
I made plans and changed my plans to prevent
My wealth flowing into the hands of others.
My wealth profited me not, nor others.

When I was a farmer, I overburdened
My beast of burden during the harvest,
And underfed them during the downtime.
I did not fallow my fields long enough,
For them to regain their fertility,
Yet expected more crop than they could yield.

When I was a merchant, I trimmed off my
Principles to fit my profit margin.

When I was a high priest, I considered
Myself high above my congregation.
I gave the impression that I had powers,
And was closer to the gods than they were.
I asked them to give and I just received.

When I was a king, I pulled up my roots
In order to get away from the people,
And tried to replant them into the heavens.
The higher I reached the lower I sank.

My sins drowned me and my innocent people.
I returned as Meshech, grand son of Noah,
I rebuilt and recolonized Kayseri.

5. I Am a Hittite

In time my language evolved to Hittite.
I began to call myself a Hittite.
I was King Anitas, I perfected
The commerce and ruled over it between
The Mediterranean and the Black Sea.
I and my people prospered; my pride swelled,
And I built Kanesh as my capital
And surrounded it with protective high walls.

I was peaceful but not without prejudice.
I did not allow the Assyrians
To live, or do business in the walled city.

I set myself on my ceremonial
Throne and gathered my generals, soldiers,
War-horses, and chariots around me.
I was also the talented sculptor.
I captured these images upon the cliffs
For you and your grandchildren to behold.

You may touch the weapons of my soldiers,
Since time has blunted the tips of their spears,
You can't be pierced. Since the ages took off
The edges of their swords, you can't be cut.

I was also an Assyrian man.
I built my house, my shop, and my warehouses
At the outside of the walls of Kanesh,
But I held the kingdom's trade in my hands.
I mined the rich silver mines of Akdag.
I exported silver; imported tin.

I was the scribe. I wrote my transactions
On clay tablets, and kept them to this day.
My tablets are open for your audit,
As you can confirm, I cheated no one.

I was the foundry man. I poured my molten
Bronze into carefully prepared clay molds
To create images like gods and goddesses.
You do not have to worship my images,
Though you can prize them as a work of art.

I was the Hittite prince Hittasides.
Being power-hungry, I fought with my
Brother Kurbanos to grab the absolute
Power, but I lost. Being a poor loser,
I burnt Kanesh and reduced it to ashes.
I meant to leave no evidence behind.
Yet my weapon of my choice betrayed me.
Intense heat double baked my clay records,
And saved them to this day for you to read.
My impulsive offense speaks for itself.

I don't expect you to learn from my crime.
As I learned nothing from the examples
Of other people who lived before me.

6. I Am a Cappadocian

Unbeknown to me, my language evolved.
This time I began to converse in Greek.
And I called myself a Cappadocian.
I was the king; I chose Mazaca as
My capital. I allied with Romans,
As any powerful ally would do,
They annexed my kingdom as a province,
And the Emperor Claudius renamed
My capital, Caesarea Mazaca.

I lost my throne, but I did not grow idle.
I kept myself busy by carving houses,
Churches, and cities into the soft stones
Of Cappadocia for you to visit.

I was St. Basil of Caesarea Mazaca.
I redefined the basic principles
Of Christianity, as they're known now.

I was the Greek youngster, I served the wine.
I was also the old Roman General.
When the cupbearer poured the wine, I gulped.

7. I Am a Byzantine

When the Roman Empire grew over-ripened
And split in two like a watermelon,
I began to call myself a Byzantine.
But Byzantine politics did not lure me.
Instead, I nurtured my natural talents
To become the shrewd merchant of Kayseri.

I passed down my trade secrets to my heirs.
Even today outsiders are not privy
To my trade secrets, but they know that
My secret teachings are not forgotten,
For their impact comes through in the success
Of the present day's Kayserian merchants.

8. I Am a Turkish Frontiersman

I was the Oguz and Afsar herdsman.
I led my herds into Byzantine lands
Through the high passes, and I let my herds
Fatten upon the green alpine pastures.
I chased the green grass season after season.

My team of powerful Anatolian
Dogs kept away the fierce wolves from my herds.
And I kept away the cities' youth and their
Corrupting ways from my sons and daughters.

I was the Kizik mountaineer, and settled
Down at the highlands of Mt. Erciyes.
I also conquered the other highlands
Of Anatolia without fighting,
I peacefully coexisted with the Greeks.

9. I Am a Seljuk Turk

I was Alpaslan, the king of Seljuks.
I crossed the borders of Byzantine
At broad day light without any concern.
I defeated the Emperor Romanus
IV Diogenes, and opened the gates
For the Turks to live in Anatolia.
I was overwhelmed by my victory.
Diogenes was humbled by defeat.

I was also a Seljuk Turkish soldier.
I was proud of being victorious,
Though I was lost in my just acquired country.

I was an independent Oguz girl.
Being isolated from cities' youth,
I was leading a fugitive-like life.
I came down from the highlands to welcome
The lost soldier. We settle at the town.

Once more, I started to read Oguz Epics,
And I'd leisure time to write new epics.

I was the stone cutter and the mason.
I built many mosques without an image.
Instead, I carved the flowers of highlands
On the altars where I knelt and worshiped.

I was a young crusading soldier passing
Though Anatolia, and heading south
To Jerusalem. My heavy armor
Was impenetrable, but it was also
A portable hell under the hot sun,
And my steed was powerful but clumsy.

I was also a Seljuk warrior,
Dressed in silk and armored lightly to keep
Cool and to maintain my agility.
My horse was bred and raised in the highlands.
It was sure-footed, for the ground under
Its hooves was its native Anatolia.
It could outmaneuver and outrun any
Newcomer horse of any crusader.
I was more effective as a Seljuk
Soldier, for I was fighting for my home.

I was the Seljuk Queen Hunat Hatun.
I started to build my monuments by
Building a bathhouse; my crew had to bathe
In order to cleanse their bodies and souls
Before they could touch their hands to building
Supplies that were to be used to build my
University, library, and mosque.

As I rest at the center of holy grounds,
I still keep learning and I pray for you.

I was the princess Gevher Nesibe.
I built the medical school and hospital
To heal the sickness of the mind and body.
When I lost Gulbahar, my only daughter,
In my grief, I said, "The death is unjust."

I commissioned Dr. Hekimoglu,
To find a remedy to prevent death,
The robber of all times, so the people
Could live their lives without the fear of death.

Hekimoglu said, "I would like to work
On this project, but I have one condition."
I said, "Sir, when you find the cure for death,
Then I'll comply with any condition."

He took off with forty mules and searched for
Remedies for forty days and forty
Nights in the highlands of Mt Erciyes.
Then he returned with forty mules loaded
Down with bundles of herbs and minerals.

In his laboratory, he and his team
Researched for forty days and forty nights.
He then came out of his lab with a small
Flask in his hand, and gave it to me saying,

"Madam, here is the cure for death, and my
Condition is that you should be the first
One to take the cure." I took the flask and
Shattered it and I told Dr. Hekimoglu
Not to duplicate his experiment."

I was the king, for my city's defense,
I restored the outer city walls as
Well as the inner castle of Kayseri.
When I was feeling safe, I came down upon
My town with the wrath of Mongolians.
I fought at outer walls and inner walls.
I killed and was killed but lost the battle.

As a Mongolian Khan, I was angry
With the tenacity of Kayserians
In defense of their city and citizens.
When I was victorious, I massacred
Most of the population without mercy
To teach them the virtue of being pliant.

I must have been a plebeian teacher,
And must have given misleading lectures.

My recently subjugated subjects
Slowly grew daringly disobedient.
They reorganized and defeated me.
I found my head at the end of a spear.
To my surprise, I saluted my death.
However, I taught nothing and learned nothing.

10. I Am an Ottoman

In time, I called myself an Ottoman.
On the surface, it looked as if it were
The easiest change I have ever made.
I spoke Turkish and went to the same mosque.

I was also a Christian Kayserian,
As before, I read my bible in Turkish,
And I attended to the same old church.

I was a farmer. At each harvest time
Tax collector came by to collect.
As before, I'd no cash to pay my taxes.
He confiscated ten percent of my crops.

I was also a merchant, and I had
New markets to sell my goods, and I prospered.
When the tax collector came, I paid my
Taxes in cash, I received my receipt,
He left me alone; I made more money.

I was a coffeehouse philosopher.
I sipped the same old black Turkish coffee.
Though it did not have the same old aroma.
I smelt something unsound with the changes.

The governor was an appointee
Who worked for the benefit of the central
Government, not for the Kayserians.
Capitals became the Rome of Ottomans,
And Kayseri became an outlying

Provincial city without cultural
Or administrative autonomy.

My taxes went to capital cities:
Bursa, Edirne and then to Istanbul,
Then trickled back to pay the salaries
And fringe benefits of the bureaucrats.

No money was being allocated
For educational institutions.
Medical school and hospitals were closed.
When I lodged my plaints with the governor,
He said, "We have fine universities
In the capital, send your young ones there."
By the time I could raise funds to send them,
The army already drafted my youth.

I was a young man and a proud soldier
In the Ottoman military forces.
I fought on the three continents to build
A great empire in the three continents.
I was happy to be an Ottoman.

I chose to colonize Southern Europe
From Crimea to the gates of Vienna.
I treated my subjects fairly and justly.

I did not present myself as a Turk,
But as an Ottoman. I told them that
They're also an Ottoman just like myself.

I did not interfere with their religion,
Language, local customs, and traditions.
I gave them equal opportunities,
When they were gifted, I promoted them
Up to Viziership, and they performed well.

A Serbian descendant family
Of viziers' able administration

Kept my empire powerful and prosperous
For an additional two centuries.

I was Mimar Sinan. I left Kayseri
When I was merely a youth to study,
And then to build my gravity defying
Monuments and mosques in the three continents.
Even today you see my bridges standing
Solid next to the crumbling new bridges.
I designed the *Suleymaniye Mosque*
To honor Suleyman the Magnificent.

In search of a site, I stood at the shores
Of the Golden Horn. I lifted my eyes,
And saw the green hill that deserved a crown.
I chose to bedeck her crest with a mosque.

I laid down the foundation of the mosque
At the shore, one mile below the crest.

My laborers, stone cutters, artisans,
Masons and assistant architects were
Enthusiastic about the project.

We worked for years to complete the foundations,
And the ground works. The morale of the crew
Was still high, for they were paid handsomely.

When the walls of the mosque were only five
Feet above the ground, I stopped the construction,
Dismissed the crew, and I slipped out of town.

Suleyman was growing old by the day.
He was anxious to get his mosque constructed.
If he wanted, he could have hired thousands
Of architects to finish the project.
Instead, he searched for me for seven years.

His secret service men found me in Baghdad.
When we arrived in Istanbul, I was

Taken directly to his audience.
I said, "Your highness, both of us prefer
To finish your mosque as soon as possible,
But it couldn't have been built sooner.
Since the foundation was not settled yet,
It couldn't have borne the weight of the mosque.
I don't want to build it for years to come,
I want it to witness the judgment day."

When I finished the mosque, I invited
Suleyman to obtain his approval
Before it was opened to the faithful.

He lifted his eyes for a split second,
Then lowered his upper eyelids as though
He were in a trance; on the holy grounds
He walked with light steps not to shake the grounds.

When he humbly entered the mosque, he did
Not march triumphantly to the altar.

Lest pride of giving sets upon his heart.
He knelt just pass the entrance door and prayed.

He knew how to celebrate an achievement.
He also knew that certain occasions
Had nothing to do with winning but giving.
He was now offering a gift to God,
And to the faithful. Shall it be received?

I knew that he was well pleased with my feat,
When he said, "Sinan, you have surpassed all
The architects of the past and the future.
Now it is the time to surpass yourself.
Draw plans for a mosque that'll be in your name.
Go to my treasurer and take the gold
And the silver by the full wagon loads."

I realized that I was being challenged
By a poet king, not by a warrior.

By being a fellow artist, he knew
That having all the power and the money
Won't help, while one is composing a poem.

I knew a magnum opus could not be
Built by piling up silver and gold bricks.
I dived into deepest depths of my
Inner self to search and find a new way.

I calculated and found a technique
To build the largest dome ever built by
A mortal under the blue dome of God.

I perfected the art of acoustics
To a level that the congregation
Could hear the sermon of a softest speaking
Priest in any location in the mosque.
I designed the most graceful minarets,
Tall and slim, to stand guard over my mosque.
I outlined the most ornate flowers that
Were to be carved on the altar and pillars.

As a king the entire world was not large
Enough for Suleyman the Magnificent.
Nothing less than pure gold tableware were
Good enough to be used on his royal table.
As a poet, when he experienced
The moment of enlightenment, he allowed
Nothing but earthenware on his table.
Seeing that, I scaled down the plans of my
Mosque, which was to be built in Kayseri.

As a colonist, I was first a soldier
And an administrator then became
A farmer, a merchant, and a citizen.
I intermarried and mixed blood with natives.
My children felt at home where they were born.

11. Decline of the Ottoman Empire

As it had happened to every other
Great empire, all through human history,
The Ottoman Empire also grew brittle,
And fell apart as one nation after
Another regained its independence.

Those former subjects of the Ottomans,
Told me that it does not matter how many
Centuries you have lived in this country,
You and your whole family are still Turks,
And you have to return to Turkiye.

Sometimes I was lucky enough to have
A little time to sell my property
At a bargain price, and some other time
I was lucky just to come out alive.

From the Southern Europe, I walk the long
Road back to Kayseri and Anatolia.
With every return, I brought back fresh blood
To further Turkicize Anatolia,
And turned it into a true Motherland.

12. The Birth of Turkiye

After six hundred years of glorious
Existence, the Ottoman Empire collapsed.
Even the motherland was occupied.
I joined my Circassian, Kurdish, and Laz
Brothers, and sisters to fight together
Against the invaders to carve a new
Country from the remnants of an empire.
I named this new Country 'Turkiye.'
She's in the likeness of a sitting bull.
She likes to keep her head always in Europe,
And her body in Anatolia.

I should have named her, "*The Republic of*
The Eastern Thrace and Anatolia."
To make it clear that she belongs to all
People who happen to be living there.

In those difficult transitional days,
I suffered an identity crises.
I denied my Ottoman heritage.
I thought that my Ottoman tolerance
Did not promote the ideals of the Turks.
By presenting myself as an Ottoman,
I convinced no other nations
That they were the same as I, 'an Ottoman.'
They said, "We don't care what you may call yourself.
We know you are a Turk and we are not."

My national habits were hard to break.
I said to myself, now I have no reason
To hide my race to please the subject nations,
For they already have their independence.

I realize now by naming the new
Country "The Republic of Turkiye."
I was exaggerating my Turkishness.
I said, "Whoever happen to live on
This land is a citizen and a Turk."

I coined new nicknames for the old people.
I referred to Kurds as the "Mountain Turks".

LXXI.   Ethnic Problems

I am a Kurd and I am a loyal
Citizen of the Turkish Republic.
I live and work any place I choose.
I am the President of Turkiye.
I am also the Commander in Chief.

I am also a Kurdish agitator.
I want to have a piece of the land.
I am a reasonable Turk with common sense.
I want to grant his wish and say good riddance.
However, I do not know what to do
With the majority of the Kurds who
Have been living for countless generations
Next to the Turks all over Turkiye.
Would they go back to live in Kurdistan,
If ever there would be such a country,
Or would they say, "Kurdistan is mine,
But we'd like to share the rest of Turkiye?"

Did I look just at one side of the coin?
What shall I do with the Turks who are living
As the majority in the Southeast?
Shall I split the trunk of one thriving tree
And think that both halves shall live ever after?

1. I Am Omer Akoglu

I am Omer Akoglu, a Turkish
Soldier in an antiterrorist squad
By night, and a true Kurdish friend by day.

They see me not as a Turkish soldier,
But as an accomplished marathon runner
With many international victories.

As I walk down the street, youngsters would say,
"When are you going to best your own time?"
An old hunter says, "My saluki is
Getting fatter and slower, please get him
To run with you to turn him slim and fast
Like yourself, before the rabbit hunting?"

I run miles every morning and to catch
My breath I sit on my favorite rock.
I then pay a visit to Mehmet's farm
To make small talk over a cup of tea,
And to enjoy another's fellowship.

2. I Am Mehmet Dagoglu

I am Mehmet Dagoglu, a young Kurd.
I am blessed with a fair wife and twin boys.
I am a terrorist under duress
By night and a dirt farmer by day.

One night my liaison came to my house,
And told me, "We have to kill somebody,
Whose name must be well known among the Turks.
To kill him by a sniper is not shocking.
We must blow his body to pieces
By a bomb to make a statement that no
One is immune to violence through being
Well-liked among the uncommitted Kurds.

"The man who is to be killed is Omer,
And you are the man who has to do it,
For you are his friend and you know his habits."

He left several land mines at my house,
For me to plant them at the path of Omer.

The next day, when Omer stopped at my farm,
I cut short our usual conversation,
And told him that there's a plot on his life.

I advised him to leave the town today,
For tomorrow might prove be too late.
I said, "You'll be rotated in a few
Short weeks from the Southeastern Turkiye
To the Western Turkiye; you could say,
'I twisted my ankle, if I cannot
Be treated at Gulhane Hospital
In Ankara, then I cannot compete
In the upcoming meet of the Army.'
It'll work. The army needs you in its team."

Omer replied, "I do not run away,
But I run towards the finishing line."

A couple of nights later, my liaison
Dropped in to interrogate me regarding
The delay of the intrigue; I had to say,
"I've been setting the mines on Omer's path
But lately he has been changing his path."

He said, "I am not here to hear your fibs.
I don't want to talk about you being
A reluctant member of the brigade.
You are useful to us because you can
Get lost in a crowd. The Turkish detectives
Would think you are a loyal citizen.

"Do I need to remind you that you have
No personal identity or life.
I know you can sacrifice your own life.
Can you sacrifice your family's life?

"As a member of the organization,
We've no present, but we may have a future.
For this future we must kill or be killed.
We rely on hatred and intolerance,

Blind faith, and single-hearted allegiance.
If you call this fanaticism, so be it."

He took my wife and boys as hostages.
Before he left the house he added, "We have
Already killed thousands of Kurdish wives,
Children, fathers, and mothers for the cause.
If you can't get a result by tomorrow,
Your wife and children will be executed.
That won't be the only consequences
Of your disobedience; it'll include
Your entire extended family.
As to your own fate, the best you can hope
For is a quick death by a firing squad."

When I was alone, I tried not to think,
For any thought that came to my mind did
Not encourage me to carry out
The atrocity that I was assigned.

If I were a Kurd, by killing a friend,
I would be violating a long honored
Kurdish code of ethics of loyalty.
If I were a terrorist, how could I
Further my cause? Turkish forces would
Take a moment to salute a fallen
Comrade in arms and the next moment they
Will arch their backs to take more drastic actions.

So I did not think, and I did not feel like
A person with a conscience of my own.
Like a robot, programmed to do a task,
I buried the mines around Omer's rock.

I could not sleep. When I heard the mine's blast,
I notified the nearest gendarme station.
They rushed his blown body to the regional
Armed Forces Hospital at Diyarbakir.
There was not much that the surgeons could do.
They stopped the profuse bleeding of his wounds,

And transferred him by air ambulance
To Gulhane Hospital in Ankara.

A medical bulletin from Gulhane
Hospital on TV stated that
What was left of Omer was his strong heart.
His prognosis for survival was nil.

When a person's body is exploded,
Medical science can't put the pieces
Together, like a jigsaw puzzle yet.

I am still leading a robotic state
Of existence and can't come out of it.
I'm not cheered by my family reunion,
Nor do I have a feeling of remorse.

3. Nightmares of Mehmet

The sleep is the worst. I see the same dreams.
I go nine hundred years into the past.
It's a time that Jerusalem was lost
To the Crusaders, and they were trying
To expand their kingdom beyond the Palestine.

After that loss, the Syrian fugitives
Diffused their consternation and sorrow;
The qadi of Damascus tore his beard
In Baghdad in the presence of the caliph,
And the whole divan shed tears of helplessness.
But the commander of the faithful could
Not take action for the power was not
In his hands to combat for the faithful.
The power was in the hands of the Turks,
And they followed their ancient common laws.

4. *Noureddin of the Zangid Turks of Syria*

First Zangid Turks consolidated their
Unlimited power over Syria,
Then over Mesopotamia
And they subdued the martial Kurdish tribes.

They captured the city of Edessa,
And recovered from the Franks their conquests
Beyond the churning waters of Euphrates.

To unite the whole Islamic powers,
Noureddin lured the wandering dervishes
And armed them with a list of crusaders'
Misdeeds committed against the Muslims.
The crusaders' worst offence was their practice
Of intercepting the Muslim pilgrim
Caravans on their journey to Mecca
And ransoming them for their families.

The dervishes traveled from one village
To the next and incited the people.
And in turn they influenced their local
Chiefs in favor of the Islamic cause.

Noureddin gradually united all
The Islamic powers, added the Kingdom
Of Damascus to that of Aleppo.
He spread his reign from the Nile to the Tigris.

The holy warrior revived the zeal
And simplicity of the first caliphs.
Gold and silk were banished from his palace,
And the use of wine from his dominions.

Public money was scrupulously
Applied to the public works and services.
His frugal household was maintained with his
Legitimate income from his three shops.

The Latins themselves were compelled to own
The wisdom, courage and even the justice,
And piety of their adversary.

5. Noureddin Summons his Kurdish Vassal Ayub

Noureddin summoned his Kurdish vassal
Ayub for the good cause. Ayub reported
With a band of skilled soldiers, his brother
Shiracouh, and his young son Saladin.
The Turks gave equal opportunity
To the Kurds, in civil life as
Well as in military services.

Noureddin recognized the genius
In Saladin and personally
Tutored and groomed him for the future roles
By instilling in him his honesty,
Loyalty, and his magnanimity.
These rare qualities elevated both
Men to the level of hero and saint.

Noureddin sent an army of twelve thousand
Turks and eleven thousand Arabs to
Egypt under the command of Shiracouh.
Although, the Turks could not capture Egypt,
For crusaders came to help the Egyptians,
And two armies were stronger than their forces.
Yet Saladin proved to be a leader
By the defense of Alexandria.

An honorable capitulation and
Retreat concluded. The Turks reserved their
Powers for a more propitious occasion.

That moment came sooner than they expected.
For Almaric, king of Jerusalem,
Was allured with the riches of Egypt,

And thought that she was ready for conquering.
He broke his treaty with Egypt by saying,
"No faith should be kept with the foes of God."

The Muslims turned their eyes towards the Turks.
Noureddin mobilized an army led by
Shiracouh and Saladin accompanied.

The crusaders prudently did not want
An engagement with the Turks in the midst
Of a hostile country, and Almaric
Retired into Palestine with the shame
That adheres to unsuccessful injustice.

After that deliverance, Shiracouh
Was invested with a robe of honor,
Which he stained with the blood of hapless Shawer.

6. Saladin Becomes the Master of Egypt

For a while Turkish emirs condescended
To hold the high office of grand vizier.
When Shiracouh died, the office
Of the grand vizier was bestowed on Saladin.
Soon he became the master of the Egypt
And said, "Since God gave me the land of Egypt
I knew that he meant Palestine for me."

Before long his master Noureddin died
And left the field open for Saladin
To unify the Muslims under himself.

7. Provocation by the Christians and the Capture of Jerusalem

To start a war, Saladin needed Christian
Provocation. He had not long to wait.
Reynald de Chatillon plundered a hoard

Of pilgrims on their way to Mecca.
He joined with some Red Sea pirates to raid
The ports which served Medina and Mecca.
A boat full of pilgrims on their voyage
To the shrine of the Ka'aba was sunk.

Reynald repeated the outrage by raiding
Another caravan bound for Mecca,
And taking its survivors, including
A sister of Saladin, into his
Castle at Kerak for ransom and saying,
"Let your Mohammed come and rescue you."

These scornful words were the cause of the fall
Of the shaky Kingdom of Jerusalem.

Saladin had massed an army of twelve
Thousand horsemen, eleven thousand more foot
Soldiers, and a body guard of a thousand
Mamelukes from Egypt, and the Turks, Arabs
And Kurds joined his already strong army.

If strategy was the strength of Saladin,
Aggression was the weakness of the Christians.
Saladin decided to actuate
An attack from his Christian enemies.
He took the city of Tiberias,
And at once besieged the wife of the Count
Of Tripoli in Count's own citadel.

He arranged his army behind the *Twin
Peaks of the Horns of Hattin* in a green
Fertile plain backed by the Lake Tiberias.
To fight him, the Christian Army would have
To advance across a waterless valley.
The question was, would the bait be taken?

Two armies fought at the Horns of Hattin
Where Jesus Christ was supposed to have preached
The Sermon on the Mount against warfare.

Muslims won a decisive victory,
Which opened the roads to Jerusalem.

8. Saladin Enters Jerusalem

Saladin entered Jerusalem
On Friday 2 October, the same day
That Mohammed had mounted from *the Sacred*
Rock on Mount Moriah to the Seventh Heaven,
Which was also the Shrine of Abraham.

The Dome of the Rock had been profaned by
Raising the cross above it, and pretending
That it was the Temple of Solomon.

The first aspiration of Saladin
In Jerusalem was to renew it
As a lasting Muslim holy city.

I was not satisfied with his mission.
I asked his permission to raze the Church
Of the Holy Sepulchre and plough other
Christian churches and chapels into the soil.

He fixed his eyes on me and recited
The following verses from the Quran.

"And Zakaria and John,
And Jesus and Elias:
All in the rank
Of the righteous." [1]

He added, "If the source is pure but its
Water's foul down stream, do we blame the source?
Regardless how sinful some man might

---

[1] Quran, 4/85

Act in the name of Jesus, we must not
Forget that he is a prophet of Islam."

The golden crosses were cast down from over
The Dome of the Rock and al-Aqsa Mosques.
And the golden crescents raised on their domes.
All of the Christian symbols were removed,
And the walls of the mosques washed with rose water.

A great service of thanksgiving was held.
Soon after the service, at the courtyard
Of the mosque, Saladin blessed his soldiers,
When it was my turn to be blessed, he said,

"You must learn to keep your sword in its scabbard
When the fighting is resolved in the field."

When the Crusaders had captured the City,
They had added exclusion to genocide,
Forbidding the presence of any Jew,
Or any Muslim within the walled City.
Now Saladin returned the compliment.
Frankish and Latin Christians were forbidden
In the City since they owed allegiance
To Rome, but Greek Orthodox Christians looking
To the Patriarch in Constantinople
And Copts, and other Christians, and Jews were
Permitted to live in Jerusalem.

9. Third Crusaders and Richard

A third Crusade set off for the re-conquest
Of Jerusalem with combined forces
Of France and England aided by fleets from
Pisa and Genoa to land at Acre.

A third and more dangerous force, the German
Emperor, Frederic Barbarossa,
Set off with more than fifty thousand men

Through Anatolia, however, he drowned
In Cilicia and his son reached Acre
Eventually with just two thousand men.

King Richard being too energetic
And too relentless with a royal code
Of dignity was a dare to Saladin.

Philip Augustus of France and Richard
Of England had their national interests,
But they were united in their resolve
To take Acre before they advanced on
The Holy City. After a siege of two
Years, they were able to overcome three
Thousand heroic defenders of Acre.
They spared their prisoners for a large ransom.

When Philip returned to France, leaving his
Forces behind, King Richard ordered all
His Muslim prisoners to be beheaded
In public, because Saladin delayed
In sending the ransom and the True Cross.
And so, through his barbarity, King Richard
Rekindled the fires of the holy war.

10. The Stalemate in War and the Birth of Legends

The following wars gave no victory
To either side, but provided legends.
The memory of Richard, Coeur de Lion,
Was forever dear to his English subjects;
And at the distance of sixty years his
Glory was celebrated in well known
Aphorisms by the grandsons of the Turks
And Saracens against whom he had fought.

During a cold winter the armies slept,
But in the spring the Franks advanced within

A day's march of Jerusalem under
The leading standard of the English King:
The Muslims were delivered by the sudden,
And miraculous retreat of the Christians.

When Richard returned to Acre he heard
That Jaffa was surprised by the Muslims.
He set sail with some merchant vessels, and leaped
Foremost on the beach: the castle was saved
By his presence; and sixty thousand Turks
And Saracens fled before his arms??

The discovery of Richard's weakness
Provoked the Turks to return in the morning,
And they found him boldly encamped before
The gates with only three hundred archers,
And seventy knights, without counting their numbers,
King Richard sustained their countercharges
And grasping his lance, he rode along their
Front, from the right flank to the left wing,
Without meeting an adversary who
Dared to encounter his deadly career??

King Richard became ill and Saladin
Himself appeared in the Christian barracks
In the disguise of a physician sent
By the Sultan to Richard whom he healed??

11. Back to the Realities of Life

In reality, the fierce war between
The Muslims and Christians was a stalemate.
King Richard had to return to England,
And the other rulers of Europe had
To go back to rule their domains before
They could press the war on Jerusalem.

The Muslim emirs had also lost their
Appetite for war, but not Saladin.

He said, "Unlike other princes, I don't
Choose a life of ease to the Holy War."
His adviser, al-Fadel, had warned him
That nobody would follow him right now.
He might summon them in the name of God,
And they would come, but they thought he was calling
On them for his own glory and ambitions.

Both sides had to reach a truce to return
To their bases to renew their resources.

12. Both Sides Win by Compromising

Saladin allowed the Crusaders to pray
In Jerusalem and hold Latin mass
In the Church of the Holy Sepulchre
As well as Greek Rite. King Richard could not
Capture Jerusalem, but he did ensure
That Europeans could thenceforth worship
In the places where Christ had lived and died.

The warfare in Palestine had promoted
A mutual acceptance and a form
Of coexistence among the people
Who once beheaded each other under
The influence of religious fanaticism.

After learning religious tolerance
The hard way, Latin, Frankish and Greek Christians
And Jews worshiped peacefully in the Muslim
City of Jerusalem dominated,
Once again, by the Dome of the Rock Mosque,
Under the crescent rather than the cross.

13. Retribution of Mehmet

I wake up with a disappointment,
For I received no blessing from Saladin.

H. I. Mavioglu

I say to myself all through the ages
There had been divisive fanaticism,
Yet some men were able to go beyond
Ethnic and national issues to unite
The people at the point of coupling creed.

I was proud of Saladin who started
As a modest Kurd at the shores of Tigris
And gradually overflowed to the Nile.
He brought together the Turks and Saracens
Not as a Kurd but in the name of God.
How far could he have gone if it were not
For the nurturing of Turkish Noureddin?
How tangled are the fates of these two people?

My mind left the safety of past behind
And forced to face the unsolved current problems.

I have an impulse to visit Omer,
But don't know what I could say to him
Or to his family if and when we meet.

Eventually, I gathered enough courage
To take the journey that I had to take.
When I arrived at Ankara, he was
Surrounded by his family and friends.
In the hospital room, the only sound
Was the puffing sound of a respirator.
He was going through the dying process.

Strangely, I felt better for a moment,
For I was not obliged to talk to Omer.
When I looked upon the faces of his
Parents, a chilling fear went through my spine.

Shall I continue to present myself
As a grieving friend of their dying son?
Or shall I have the guts to tell the truth?
If I can find the courage to confess
Shall I find the proper words to utter?

His mother, Aysel, is just like the earth
Of Anatolia that cloaks the seeds
Against the bitter colds of the winter.
When the warm spring sun smiles upon the earth,
She lets the seeds sprout then to grow deep roots
In order to protect themselves against
The drought under the scorching summer sun.
She is a typical mother who teaches
Her son to be peaceful, though she accepts
The fact that his son must serve his country.

As the Anatolian earth welcomes
Each rain drop as a favor from the heavens,
She endures the pain of a fallen son
As a guarantee for a peaceful future.
I would have been proud if she were my mother.

His father, Isa, is like the scrub oak
Of the craggy hills of Mt. Erciyes.
What one sees of that oak above the ground
Is small in comparison to its roots.
He is small, scraggy, and close to the ground.
If he were to fall, he'd not fall too far
For the ground stands nearby to break his fall.
Just like the scrub oak he must have deep roots
In the hearts of the people around him.

Isa is a giver not a receiver,
Yet the people showered respect on him.
What's more, respectfully they addressed him
As *Usta Isa*, meaning Master Isa.
I preferred to call him "Master Uncle."

After Omer died and the respirator
Was turned off an eerie silence lingered.
As his parents and relatives came out
Of the room, one could not hear subbing nor
See weeping for their throats and eyes went dry.

He was buried with a military
Ceremony—flags, bands and gun salute.

14. Confession of Mehmet

When the people left the cemetery,
I sidled next to Isa and asked for
An appointment for a private talk
About his son. He said, "I will be here
Tomorrow at sunset to tidy the grave
And to say a prayer when *the hidden*
Veil is lifted from the face of heavens."

I went early and paced between the graves,
I read the epitaphs upon the tombstones,
Tried to calm my nerves and searched for the right
Words to say, as if there were right words for
A devastating occasion like this.
I could find no words that could make it less
Disheartening for either one of us.

Master Isa shoved up right at sunset.
He picked up the weeds, and smoothened the earth
With his bare hands with a care of a father
Who'd straighten out the wrinkles of bed-sheets
Before putting his toddler son to sleep.

When the reddish western skies turned light gray,
He closed his physical eyes to focus
On his inner vision and said a prayer.
Then he said, "It's getting dark, let's go
To a teahouse; you've a few words to say."
I said, "It won't take long. I'll say it here."

Then I pulled my gun out of its holster,
Cocked its hammer and handed it to him
Saying, "While you hear my story, you have
The right and my consent to pull the trigger
At any moment and to walk away."

He listened without uttering a word,
Or asking questions, or moving, except
His hands moved just to brush away his tears.

When I finished, Isa with trembling hands
Took the bullets out of the gun, and handed
To me both the empty gun and the bullets.

We sat there for a while without moving
As if we were afraid to wake up Omer.

15. Master Isa Talks

After composing himself, he started
To talk as if to himself. His voice startled
Me for it sounded not like a man's voice,
But like an echoing sound from a cave.

"Bloodstain can't be cleansed with blood but with water.
One can't extinguish the spark of terrorism
By swaddling it in a cloth of gunpowder,
But by exposing its murderous face,
And allowing people to see its ugliness,
While they breathe the fresh breath of acceptance.
Evil thrives where the goodness is dormant.
Where goodness is nurtured, there evil starves.

"God will not judge us just on the basis
Of one moment of slip, but what we had
Done with our moments all through our life times.
Shall I judge a man just on the basis
Of what he's committed under duress?
Shall I ever forget one thousand years
Of brotherhood and judge the majority
For the misdeeds of a few troublemakers?

"My father fought at Gallipoli with
His Kurdish buddy against the English
And Anzacs, risking their lives for each other.

"I served at peacetime. The only difference
Between the Turkish and Kurdish soldiers
Was our regional drawl, and we were lumped
Together as Anatolian boys,
Compared to the soldiers from Istanbul
And other European provinces.

"For years my customers, from the Kurdish
Villages towed their tractors to my shop.
I'd fix them by using old parts or by
Manufacturing parts in my workshop,
For those parts are not listed in catalogs.
They'd ask how much they owed me, I'd tell them,
And they'd drive away. The next harvest time
They'd stop at my workshop to pay their debts.
I'll continue my dealings as before."

When it was completely dark, he stopped talking.
The silence of the night intensified,
And the daytime's sounds took an eerie tone.
A dog' howling sounded like a ghost's groaning.
Carefree love songs of the crickets and frogs
Grew into a pitch of plea to their mates.
Then the night revealed its eternal self.
The distant stars appeared to be nearby,
As if one could touch them with a long ladder.

The moon rose once more over the eastern
Skies with a human face to radiate
Its light of hope upon the gloomy earth.

Master Isa must have seen a faint gleam
Of hope in the future. Once more he spoke,
"My son owed service to his country,
And paid the price but no state owns his bones.
I know he'll be at peace at his birthplace.

When I go back I'll build a memorial
And relocate his remains to rest there."

I sensed an opportunity in his
Plan for me to try to redeem myself.
I offered my service for his project.
He said that he knows where the best granite
Beds are at Mt. Erciyes and he could
Cut them as if they were a lump of candy,
And mold the metals as if they were plastic,
But he'd need help with writing the epitaph.

I was so anxious to do anything
At all that I volunteered to write it.
He advised me regarding its contents
And I came up with the following verse:

"The Turks and Kurds always fought side by side
For the liberty of the Motherland.
In peacetime or wartime they had allied
For they meant to go forward hand in hand.

Nowadays a friend is killing his friend.
Shall this frightful fratricide ever end?"

LXXII. The Questions of Yasar and the Answers of Adem

Yasar was going back regularly
To his rendezvous without finding Adem.
When the people questioned him regarding
The whereabouts of the Doctor, he felt
They were saying, 'What did you do to him?'
Adem could have fallen from one of many
Cliffs, and Yasar himself might be a prime
Suspect for pushing Adem to his death.

The next dawn, Yasar went to Mt. Erciyes
And located Adem at the north rim
Of the sanctuary of Akgelin.
His blinkless eyes were fixed on the void.

Yasar said, "Doc, I know you asked me not
To search for you. When you would complete your
Pilgrimage you would come down on your own.
I could not wait any longer for you
To keep our rendezvous; I had my doubts
If you were ever going to return.
Do you have any conception of time?
Do you know how long you'd been on this mountain?

"Since we met I've been trying to understand
You, but you proved to be an enigma,
Because the background information I
Have collected on you does not add up.

You say, you are a native Kayserian,
Though your historical facts are factual,
You don't still pass for a man of this era.

"When you talk of the future who can judge,
Whether your prophecies shall come to pass?
When you talk of the blurred past who can prove
Or deny that what you say is right or wrong?

You sound like a man from the labyrinths
Of the distant past, or from the future.
Please tell me what is your identity?"

Adem replied, "There is no mystery
About the identity of mankind.
All of them emanate from the same source
And all of them return to the same source.
The Self shrouds its body and brain and goes
Back to the Earth. The Soul returns to God.

"Life has been my first gift, which still thrills me
With its pain and pleasure, gloom and gladness,
Tears and laughter, losses and wins or draws.

"The Noncancelable itinerary
Of our journey was written before we
Were born and it simply starts with our birth
But it will not end because of our death,
Unless the Soul and the Self were connected
With each other in a *seamless Oneness*.

"All through my lives, I have learnt many things,
Also I have forgotten many things.
Yet one thing I knew from the beginning:
I came from the Eternity and I
Am journeying to the Eternity.

"Between the Eternity and the worldly
Life there's a veil. It's so thin, yet so strong.
Several times I have touched that thin veil,

But my invisible shells were so thick,
So heavy that I could not go through it.
Now I come naked like a newborn baby;
I am fit to join the Eternity."

LXXIII. Appendix I

Comparative List of Place Names

A
Adramyttium, Edremit
Attalia, Antalya

B
Black Sea, Kara Deniz
Bosphorus, Istanbul Bogazi
Byzantium, Istanbul

C
Caesarea Mazaca, Kayseri
Constantinople, Istanbul

D
Dardanelles, Canakkale Bogazi

E
Edessa, Urfa
Euphrates River, Firat
Euxiene Sea, Black Sea, Kara Deniz

H
Halicarnassus, Bodrum,
Hellespont, Dardanelles, Canakkale Bogazi

K
Kanesh, Nesa, Kultepe

L
Lesbos, Mytilene, Midilli Adasi

M
Mazaca, Kayseri
Mt. Argaeus, Erciyes Dagi
Mt. Ida, Kaz Dagi
Mt. Olympus, Uludag
Myra, Demre

P
Sinope, Sinop
Smyrna, Izmir

T
Taurus Mountains, Toros Daglari
Tigris River, Dicle
Trebizond, Trabzon
Tubal, Kayseri

0-595-30556-3

Printed in Great Britain
by Amazon

23796591R00148